Non-Vegetarian Delights

Published by
Lotus Press

Non-Vegetarian Delights

Sandhya Kumar

4735/22, Prakash Deep Building
Ansari Road, Darya Ganj,
New Delhi-110002

Lotus Press : Publishers & Distributors
Unit No. 220, 2nd Floor, 4735/22, Prakash Deep Building,
Ansari Road, Darya Ganj, New Delhi- 110002
Ph.: 32903912, 23280047 • E-mail : lotus_press@sify.com
www.lotuspress.co.in

Non-Vegetarian Delights

ISBN: 81-8382-115-4

Published by : **Lotus Press,** New Delhi-110002
Printed at : Concept Imprint, Delhi

The non-vegetarian dishes have occupied a significant place in Indian cooking. It is no more restricted to the Mughlai cuisine. People now have developed a taste for other non-vegetarian dishes such as prawns and shrimps. The secrets of non-vegetarian dishes unfold in this unique collection of non-vegetarian recipes. These are easy to make, delicious to taste, and each dish is enhanced with subtle flavours of coriander, a dash of spices, or sprinkling of cheese. The recipes include dishes containing eggs to cater to the taste- buds of egg lovers as well. This book will be a handy guide for those who love cooking and for beginners as well.

GLOSSARY OF COOKING TERMS

Batter: A mixture of flour and besan flour, a variety of other ingredients and liquid of such consistency that it can be beaten or stirred, used generally to coat foods for frying, or for making idlis and such like delicacies.

Beat: To mix ingredients together with a circular up and down motion using a whisk, spoon or an electric beater.

Blend: To stir, rather than beat, ingredients until they are thoroughly combined.

Chop: To cut into small pieces.

Crush: To pulverise by rolling with a rolling pin or by mashing until the food is of coarse powder.

Dice: To cut into small cubes.

Fry: To cook in hot fat or oil.

Garnish: To decorate a dish by adding other foodstuffs over the main dish.

Grate: To reduce food like some vegetables or cheese by rubbing them on sharp cutting teeth of a grater.

Grease: To rub fat or oil on the surface of vessels.

Knead: To work dough by pressing it with the heels of the hands, folding and turning it and pressing it until it has been worked into a contained elastic texture.

Mash: To soften and breakdown food by using the hands or masher or the back of a spoon.

Mayonnaise: A thick sauce made of flour, oil, vinegar mustard powder.

Melt: To change fat and solid dissolvable foods into a liquid state by heating.

Season: To add salt, spices or other ingredients in hot oil to increase the flavours of food.

Shred: Cut in fine strips.

Simmer: To cook a liquid barely at the boiling point. The surface will show only a few bubbles breaking slowly.

CONTENTS

SOUPS AND SALADS

SOUPS AND SALADS

1. FRUIT AND CHICKEN SALAD

Ingredients

20 ml olive oil

1 lettuce

cucumber and any other

1 apple

green salad

1 pear

1 orange

1 kiwifruit

2 oz (50g) cooked and chopped

chicken breast

2 tbsps plain yogurt

1 tbsp wine vinegar

1 clove garlic, crushed

salt and freshly

ground black pepper

Method

1. Mix all the fruits.
2. Mix the dressing, pour over fruits.
3. Place them with chicken on a bed of shredded lettuce.
4. Garnish with tomato quarters, cucumber twists and lemon quarters.

2. CHEESE, PRAWN AND ASPARAGUS SALAD

Ingredients

100 gms cottage cheese

150 gms peeled prawns

4 tbsps chopped and diced cucumber

freshly ground black pepper

lettuce or watercress

200 gms asparagus tips

Method

1. Mix the cottage cheese, prawns and cucumber together.
2. Add any seasoning to taste with the pepper.
3. Lay the mixture on a bed of shredded lettuce or watercress and decorate with the asparagus tips.

3. LETTUCE & EGG SALAD

Ingredients

8 eggs

½ tsp of crushed

black peppercorn

a bunch of lettuce leaves

6 tbsps of vinegar

salt to taste

1 tsp mustard powder

½ tsp white pepper powder

2 tbsps salad oil

Method

1. Boil eggs in water for twelve minutes.
2. Cool them, peel and place in cold water.
3. Wash the lettuce leaves in running water and keep in chilled water.
4. Cut eggs into pieces.
5. Tear lettuce leaves with hand and gently mix eggs with them.
6. Make a dressing by mixing salt, white pepper powder, crushed blackpeppercorns, vinegar, mustard powder and salad oil.
7. Mix this gently with the prepared lettuce and eggs.
8. Serve cold.

4. CURRIED CHICKEN AND YOGURT SALAD

Ingredients

75 gms chicken breast, cut into cubes

125 gms yogurt

1 tsp curry powder

unlimited green salad vegetables

Method

1. Mix yogurt and curry powder together.
2. Stir in the cubes of cooked chicken.
3. Serve on a bed of fresh green salad vegetables.

5. CHICKEN SOUP

Ingredients

5 cups chicken broth

1 cup shredded
boneless chicken pieces

2 tbsps soya sauce

1 tbsp vinegar

1tbsp green chilli sauce

4 tbsps cornflour

½ tsp black pepper

2 tsps chicken masala powder

salt to taste

Method

1. Put chicken broth and chicken pieces in a pressure pan.
2. Bring it to a boil.
3. Reduce the heat and then let it cook till the chicken pieces become tender (about 25 minutes).
4. Add soya sauce, vinegar, green chilli sauce, black pepper powder, chicken masala and salt.
5. Mix cornflour in 1/4 cup water.
6. Slowly add this to the soup and stir continuously.

7. Cook until it becomes thick.
8. Remove from heat and serve hot.

6. HOT AND SOUR PRAWN SOUP

Ingredients

4 large fresh prawns

75 ml oil

2 tbsp fresh lime Juice

1tbsp coriander leaves

1 tsp sugar

1 stalk lemon grass

1 red chilli

salt to taste

Method

1. Shell and devein the prawns.
2. Heat the oil and fry the prawns.
3. Add 4 glasses of water.
4. Add the lemon grass, lime juice, sugar, salt and red chilli.
5. Cook till the prawns are done.
6. Serve into individual cups and garnish with coriander leaves.

Snacks

SNACKS

1. BREADED PEPPER CHICKEN

Ingredients

5 boneless chicken breasts

4 tbsps black soya sauce

2 tbsps ajinomoto

1- 1½ tbsps salt

4 tbsp coarsely ground pepper

dash of chilli sauce

breadcrumbs

oil for frying

Method

1. Cut chicken into thin pieces of any shape you desire.
2. Marinate them overnight with soya sauce, salt, ajinomoto, pepper and chilli sauce.
3. Roll in breadcrumbs and fry till golden brown.
4. Serve with sauce or raw salad.

2. FRENCH FRIED PRAWNS

Ingredients

16 boiled prawns

¼ cup maida

1 egg

¼ tsp baking powder

¼ cup milk

salt to taste

Method

1. Mix together the maida, baking powder, egg and salt.
2. Add enough milk to form a thick batter.
3. Dip each prawn in the batter.
4. Heat the oil and fry the prawns to a golden colour.
5. Serve hot.

3. BUTTER CHICKEN FRY

Ingredients

500 gms boneless chicken

3 tsps garam masala

2-3 tsps ginger-garlic paste

3 tsps chilli powder

1 tsps turmeric powder

3-4 tsps vinegar

3 tsps red food colour

2 tsp pepper powder

salt according to taste

4 tsps oil

½ cup cream or malai

½ cup cashewnut powder

Method

1. Marinate the chicken with the above ingredients except for cream and cashew powder for at least 8 hours or preferably overnight.
2. Put the pan on fire, add the oil.
3. When it reaches smoking point then add the chicken pieces.
4. Mix well and cover the pan with a lid.
5. When the chicken pieces are cooked then add the cream and cashewnut powder.
6. Fry until the mixture is completely dry.
7. Serve hot, garnishing it with coriander leaves .

4. CHICKEN AND VEGETABLE KABABS

Ingredients

500 gms boneless, skinless chicken

2 potatoes

2 tomatoes

2 capsicums

skewers

For the Masala

¼ cup yogurt

1 tsp ginger paste

1 tsp garlic paste

1 tsp green chilli paste

1 tsp cumin powder

1 tsp coriander powder

1 tsp aniseed

¼ tsp turmeric powder

¼ tsp garam masala

salt to taste

2 tsps lime juice

red/orange colour

Method

1. Mix all the masalas in the yogurt and keep for about 10 minutes.
2. Marinate the chicken and vegetables with the mix for about an hour and store in the refrigerator.
3. Pierce through the skewers alternate pieces of chicken and vegetable.
4. Place on a barbecue grill or bake in the oven for 15 minutes. Remove from heat and coat the pieces with the remaining marinade.
5. Keep for another 5-10 minutes in the oven until the chicken is cooked and fried well.
6. Serve hot.

5. SALTED PLAITS

Ingredients

1 cup maida

½ tsp salt

¼ tsp cuminseeds

6 tsps chilled butter

1 egg yolk

¼ tsp baking powder

milk according to need

Method

1. Mix flour, salt, baking powder and cuminseeds.
2. Rub chilled butter into it.
3. Add the egg yolk and milk to make a smooth dough.
4. Roll the dough into 1/8" thick rolls, then cut 1" wide 3" long strips.
5. Make plaite by twining 3 strips together.
6. Brush with beaten eggs.
7. Bake in moderate oven for 10 to 15 minutes or till they are golden brown.

6. EGG CHEESE BALLS

Ingredients

2 whites of egg

2 cubes cheese, grated

4 tbsps flour

½ tsp salt

½ tsp chopped green

a pinch of baking soda
2 chillies, chooped

1 tsp chopped coriander

¼ tsps mango powder leaves

1 red chilli

chaat masala

oil for frying

Method

1. Beat the egg white till stiff.
2. Add the sieved flour with all the above ingredients except oil. Mix well.

3. Heat oil on a medium heat.
4. Make balls from the dough with wet hands and deep fry till very light golden.
5. Drain on a paper and sprinkle chaat masala over them.
6. Serve at tea or cocktail.

7. CHICKEN PAKODA

Ingredients

½ kg chicken boneless

100 gms cornflour

100 gms custard powder

salt and chilli powder to taste

clove and cardamom powder

oil

Method

1. Make a semi-liquid paste of cornflour and custard powder by adding water and salt, chilli and cardamom-clove powder.
2. Mix the chicken pieces with the semi liquid paste and keep aside for 30 minutes and later fry in oil.
3. Serve hot.

8. CHICKEN TIKKA MASALA

Ingredients For Marinating

2 tsps ginger-garlic paste

¼ tsp turmeric powder

½ tsp chilli powder

1 tsp coriander powder

1 tsp garam masala

½ tsp cumin powder

salt

½ cup curd, beaten well

For the Gravy

1 onion, chopped

2 tsps tomato puree

¼ tsp turmeric powder

2 tsps coriander powder

1½ tsps chilli powder

1 tsp ginger-garlic paste

salt to taste

3 tbsps oil

½ tsp garam masala powder

coriander leaves, finely chopped

1 tsp cream (optional) for garnish

Method

1. Marinate the chicken with the ingredients given above for an hour.
2. Then put this on skewers and grill till cooked. Heat oil in a vessel, fry onions and add the ginger-garlic paste.
3. Let it fry well till the oil separates.
4. Then add all the powdered masala, and the tomato puree, salt to taste.
5. Add a little water and let the gravy thicken.
6. Then add the chicken pieces and cook for a while.
7. Finally when the gravy is thick, remove from fire.
8. Garnish with coriander leaves and cream.

9. LEMON GARLIC CHICKEN

Ingredients

600 gms chicken pieces

1 tbsp garlic paste

vinegar

100 gms cream (freshly made)

1½ tsps salt

1 tbsp oil

½ tbsp sugar

½ tsp pepper powder

pinch of red food colour

2 lemons

Method

1. Wash the chiken pieces thoroughly, and mop dry with a clean towel.
2. Add the marinade and keep aside for 1 hour.
3. Heat them over medium heat for about 15-20 minutes with the lid on.
4. When the chicken is slightly done, remove the lid and let the chicken go a little dry but not completely.
5. Add fresh lemon juice. Heat a little more.
6. Add 2 tablespoons of cream and stir a little to give the chicken a little coated look.
7. Add coarsely ground black pepper.
8. Serve with garlic bread and spicy onion salad.

10. DEVILLED EGGS

Ingredients

4 eggs, hard boiled

1 onion

2 green chillies, finely chopped

5-6 cashewnuts, finely chopped

a few raisins

5 big boiled potatoes, mashed very well

1 sprig coriander leaves, finely chopped

½ tsp sugar

salt as per taste

1 tsp cumin powder

1 tsp coriander powder

1 egg for coating

breadcrumbs for coating

oil for deep frying

Method

1. Shell the hard boiled eggs and cut them neatly in half.
2. Take out the yolks carefully.
3. To the yolks add the chopped onions, green chillies, chopped cashewnuts, raisins, chopped coriander leaves, sugar and salt and mix well.
4. Fill this mixture back in the egg white halves taking care not to break them.
5. To the mashed potato add the coriander cumin powder and salt.
6. Heat and put 2 tsp oil in it.

7. Fry the mashed potatoe till they are brown.
8. Take a fistful of this potato mix and cover one egg half with the stuffing, taking care that the potato is covered entirely.
9. Roll in the beaten egg and coat with breadcrumbs.
10. Deep fry till golden brown on all sides.
11. Serve hot with lemon wedges and onion ring.

11. EGG BREAD SCRAMBLE

Ingredients

10 slices scrambled wheat bread

4 eggs whipped neat

1 tsp besan flour

5 green chillies, finely chopped

1 onion, cut into very small pieces

1 small cup chopped coriander leaves

1 big tomato, cut into very small pieces

1 tsp chilli powder

2 tsps oil

salt to taste

Method

1. Heat oil in pan, fry the onions and green chillies.
2. Add to it the beaten egg and scramble it.
3. Add some more oil and fry well the scrambled pieces of bread.
4. Add the chilli powder, salt and tomatoes and fry till all mix well.
5. Garnish with coroamder.

12. EGG CHAAT

Ingredients

6 hard boiled eggs

1 medium-sized onion

4-5 green chillies

2 tsps chopped coriander

1 tsp ketchup

½ cup tomato sauce

1 tsp chilli powder

1 tsp chaat masala

2 tbps tamarind extract

2 tsps jaggery

salt to taste

Method

1. Make chutney by boiling tamarind and jaggery in a little water for 4-5 minutes and strain.
2. Cut the boiled eggs into quarter pieces.
3. Mix well with chopped onions, green chillies, coriander leaves, ketchup, chaat masala, chilli powder, 1 tbsp tamarind chutney and salt.
4. Serve garnished with lemon wedges and chopped coriander leaves.

13. EGG KABABS

Ingredients

4 eggs, hard boiled

2 tsps besan flour

1 onion, finely chopped

1 egg (white only)

1 tbsp mint leaves, finely chopped

1 tbsp coriander leaves, finely chopped

2 green chillies, finely chopped

¼ tsp chilli powder

salt to taste

oil for frying

Method

1. Grate the hard boiled eggs finely.
2. Combine with all other ingredients except oil.
3. Mix well and knead into a smooth dough.
4. Divide the mixture into flat round cutlets and keep aside.
5. Heat oil in a kadai and fry the kababs, until crisp and golden brown.
6. Garnish with onion rings.
7. Serve hot with mint chutney.

14. FRENCH TOAST

Ingredients

100 ml milk

3 tsps sugar

4 slices bread

1 egg

½ tsp salt

a few drops of vanilla essence

2 tsps ghee or butter

Method

1. Beat the eggs in a bowl till frothy.
2. Add the sugar, salt, vanilla essence and milk.
3. Beat the mixture till the sugar dissolves.
4. Soak the bread slices in the above mixture for just a minute.
5. Heat a non-stick pan over a low flame and butter slightly.
6. Fry the slices of bread on the pan on both sides, till brown.
7. Serve hot with honey or pancake syrup.

15. FISH CUTLET

Ingredients

2 small tins light tuna

2 large onions, finely chopped

2 tbsps ginger, finely chopped

1 tsp finely chopped garlic

5 green chillies, finely chopped

1-2 eggs, well beaten

1 small potato, boiled and mashed

3 sprigs curry leaves, finely chopped

½ tsp chilli powder

¼ tsp turmeric powder

½ tsp pepper powder

½ tsp garam masala

2 tbsps oil

breadcrumbs for coating

oil for deep frying

For the Garam Masala

2 tbsps cloves

2 tbsps cardamom

2 tbsps aniseed

3 small cinnamon sticks

Method

1. Dry roast all the garam masala ingredients, cool and powder.
2. Remove all water from the tuna, pour fresh water and discard.
3. Keep the mince aside.
4. Pour 2 tbsps of oil in a pan and saute ginger, garlic, green chillies and curry leaves on a low flame for a few seconds.
5. Add the onions and saute until transparent.
6. Add all the powders and continue to saute.
7. Add the garam masala and salt and cook until well blended.
8. Add the fish mince and cook well.
9. There should be no water in the mixture.
10. Remove and cool.
11. Mix the mashed potatoes and blend well. Shape into oval or round patties, dip in beaten egg, coat with bread crumbs and deep fry.
12. The patties can be frozen and deep fried when required.
13. Serve hot with an onion salad and mint/ tamarind chutney.

16. FISH FRY

Ingredients

3 fillets cat fish

1 large onion, cut into small pieces

1 tsp ginger-garlic paste

coriander leaves

1 tsp garam masala

1 lemon

1 tsp coconut powder

1 tsp chilli powder

1 tsp coriander powder

½ tsp turmeric powder

salt

oil

Method

1. Cut fish into 2-inch pieces and wash them well with vinegar and water.
2. Marinate the washed fish with ginger-garlic paste, salt, chilli powder, coriander powder. Add the juice of 1 lemon, mix well and marinate.
3. Keep in fridge for 24 hours or more.
4. Remove the marinated fish from fridge and squeeze out all the water.
5. Retain this water.
6. Heat a skillet and add oil into it to deep fry the fish.
7. When the oil is hot add the fish pieces one by one.
8. Turn them over slowly and gently so that they are fried eventlly till brown.
9. Take another skillet and add oil.
10. Add the onion pieces and saute.
11. After a few minutes add the ginger, chilli, garlic paste and fry them till light brown.

12. Add chilli powder, garam masala, turmeric, coconut powder and salt and fry for a few more minutes.
13. Now add the fried fish and mix slowly for 2 minutes.
14. Add the lemon juice and coriander.
15. Serve hot.

17. FISH IN GREEN MASALA

Ingredients

fish (of your choice)

small bunch coriander leaves

½ inch ginger

4 cloves garlic

4 green chillies

½ onion

¼ tsp turmeric

½ tsp chilli powder

½ tsp coriander powder

1 tsp lime

¼ tsp garam masala powder

salt

Method

1. Grind the masalas coarsely.
2. Marinate the fish with the above masalas and keep aside for 2 to 3 hours.
3. Roll each piece in breadcrumbs and fry.
4. Serve with onions and lime.

18. PRAWN PAKORA

Ingredients

10 jumbo prawns

1 tsp ginger paste

1 tsp chopped coriander

1 egg

½ cup besan

2 chopped onions

2 tsps soya sauce

2 green chilies

oil for deep frying

Method

1. Beat the egg and flour with a little oil.
2. Add the soya sauce.
3. Then add everything else into the batter and mix well.
4. Shape into flat cutlets and fry.
5. Hold down the prawn with the flat spoon or it curls back.
6. Serve with mustard sauce and green salad .

19. PRAWN TIKKA

Ingredients

500 gms grey prawns

¼ cup yogurt

1 tsp garam masala

1 tsp garlic paste

1 tsp ginger paste

1 medium lemon

1 tsp turmeric powder

salt

1 tsp chilli powder

½ tsp coriander-cumin powder

1 tbsp butter

Method

1. Wash the prawns.
2. Remove the shell and black string from the prawns.
3. Mix the prawns with turmeric powder, salt and juice of lemon.
4. Keep aside for 15 minutes.
5. Mix yogurt, garlic paste, ginger paste, garam masala, chilli powder and coriander-cumin powder into a bowl and mix with prawns.
6. Marinate the prawns for 2-3 hours.
7. Roast the prawns in barbecue grill, apply butter and roast from time to time.

20. SHRIMP CUTLET

Ingredients For Cover

2 big potatoes

½ slice bread

½ tsp pepper powder

salt

For Coating

¼ cup semolina

¼ cup rice flour

For Filling

1 cup shrimp, peeled and deveined

½ cup coconut, grated

1 cup onions, finely chopped

1 tsp chilli powder

½ tsp turmeric powder

1 tsp coriander-cumin powder

½ cup chopped coriander leaves salt

Method

1. Boil the potatoes and mash while still hot.
2. Soak a slice of bread in water.
3. Drain all water from the bread and add it to the potatoes.
4. Add pepper powder and salt.
5. Knead well and keep aside.
6. Wash and clean the shrimps.
7. Add the salt, turmeric powder and chilli powder to it.
8. Fry the chopped onions in a little oil for a minute.
9. Add the shrimps and coriander-cumin powder and fry a little more.
10. Add approximately a cup of water to it.
11. Cover the pot and let the shrimps cook for 10 minutes or so.
12. Once they are cooked increase the heat and dry the mixture.
13. Add the coconut and chopped coriander to it. Keep aside.
14. Make balls of mashed potatoes and flatten on your palm.
15. Add a spoonful of shrimp mixture to it and close the balls.
16. Flatten gently on your palm.
17. Roll it in semolina-rice flour coating and shallow fry.
18. Serve with tomato ketchup or mint chutney.

21. SPICY PRAWNS

Ingredients

½ kg prawns

½ tsp garlic paste

½ tsp tumeric powder

a few sprigs curry leaves

salt to taste

1" cinnamon

2 cloves

125 gms onions

4 tsps green chillies, ground coarsely

2 bay leaves

1 tsp lime juice

2 tsps oil

2 cardamoms

Method

1. Wash and devein the prawns well.
2. Slice the onions evenly, and cut the bay leaves into pieces.
3. Heat the oil and when very hot add the add curry leaves and bay leaves. Then add the onions.
4. Toss till the onions turn light brown.
5. Add the rest of the ingredients till the prawns are well cooked and hard.
6. Serve hot.

22. SEEKH KABABS

Ingredients

400 gms lamb mince

1 tsp chopped ginger

½ tsp chopped green chilli

½ tsp chopped coriander leaves

1 tsp garam masala powder

1 tsp chilli powder

1 tsp oil

salt to taste

Method

1. Squeeze the mutton mince in a dry cloth to remove excess water.
2. Mix all the above ingredients except oil. Knead well.
3. Divide into 8 equal portions and make balls.
4. Spread the mince balls on to the skewers, using a wet hand.
5. Press evenly to get kababs of six inches length.
6. Roast in a moderately hot tandoor for 7-8 minutes or in a pre-heated oven (175°C) for 10 minutes.
7. Brush with oil and again roast for 2 minutes.

Note : For Seekh Kababs, use mince which has been passed through a mixer twice.

23. SHAMMI KABABS

Ingredients

500 gms mince meat without fat

chana dal (washed and soaked in water for ½ hour)

2 tbsps coriander-cumin powder

10 garlic flakes

1 inch ginger piece

1 tsp garam masala

2 cardamoms

2 cinnamons

3 cloves garlic

a pinch of pepper

1 tsp chilli powder

coriander and mint chopped

1 egg

½ tsp lemon juice

1 onion, minced

salt to taste

oil/ghee

Method

1. To the washed and drained mince, add the chana dal, whole masala, 1 cup warm water, salt to taste and then cook till dry.
2. Remove from heat and add the ginger, garlic, pepper, chilli powder, coriander-cumin powder.
3. Grind to a fine paste and then form into dough.
4. To the minced onion, add the finely chopped mint, coriander, lime juice and salt to taste.
5. Beat the egg lightly. Divide the dough into lemon-sized balls.
6. Flatten each ball in the palm of your hand and stuff with a little of the onion mixture.
7. Shape into a kabab and dip in the beaten egg.
8. Shallow fry till golden.

24. GALOUTI KABAB

Ingredients

1 kg mutton mince

3 tbsps ginger paste

3 tbsps garlic paste

75 gms raw papaya

3 tbsps butter

1 tsp chilli powder

½ tsp mace powder

1 tsp green cardamom powder

4 tbsps fried grams

ghee as required

salt as required

Method

1. Wash and drain the mince and refrigerate for 15 minutes.
2. Peel and deseed the papaya, put in a blender and make a fine paste.
3. Mix all the ingredients, except the ghee with the refrigerated mince.
4. Divide into 32 equal portions, apply a little melted ghee on the palms and flatten the mince into round patties.
5. Heat ghee in a tava and shallow fry over low heat until both sides brown evenly.
6. Serve hot.

25. SHAHI MURGH KABAB

Ingredients

8 chicken breast pieces

ghee for deep frying

For the Marinade

3½ tsps ginger paste

3½ tsps garlic paste

½ tsp chilli powder

4 tbsps lemon juice

salt as required

For the Filling

300 gms paneer

8 green chillies

20 gms coriander leaves

2 pineapple rings

40 gms cashewnuts

1 tsps black cumin

½ tsp chilli powder

salt as required

For the Batter

3 eggs

150 gms cornflour

50 gms flour

salt as required

Method

1. Clean, remove the skin, debone and keep the winglet bone intact.
2. With a knife-tip make a deep slit along the thick edge of the breast, taking care not to cut the piece.

3. Open out the slit pieces and flatten with a bat.
4. For the marination mix the chilli powder, salt and lemon juice with the ginger and garlic pastes and apply this mixture to the flattened chicken breasts.
5. Keep aside for at least 30 minutes.
6. For the filling mash the paneer in a bowl, deseed and finely chop green chillies.
7. Clean, wash and chop the coriander leaves, finely chop the pineapple rings and roughly chop the cashewnuts.
8. Add these chopped ingredients, cumin, chillies and salt with the mashed paneer and mix well.
9. Place a portion of the filling in the middle of the marinated chicken breast and fold to make a ball with the bone sticking out.
10. Refrigerate for 15 minutes.
11. For the batter break the eggs in a bowl, add cornflour, flour, salt and water and whisk to make a batter.
12. Heat ghee in a pan, dip the stuffed chicken breasts in the batter and deep fry over medium heat until light golden colour.
13. For the finishing touch, grease a roasting tray with a little ghee, arrange the fried chicken breasts on it and roast in a pre-heated oven for 10-12 minutes.

26. BHUTA MASU

Ingredients

1 kg mutton

150 gms onions, sliced

100 gms tomatoes, chopped

12 sprigs spring onions

2 stalks celery

3 tsps soya sauce

a pinch of ajinomoto

1" cube ginger

a pinch of salt

½ cup oil

Method

1. Boil meat with a pinch of salt and ginger bits till the meat is tender.
2. Slice the meat into juliene strips when it is cold.
3. Heat the oil, add the ginger and onions, keep stirring till the onion is transparent.
4. Add the rest of the ingredients except the greens.
5. Fry lightly till all the moisture is absorbed.
6. Just before serving, add the tomatoes and greens.

27. MALAI KABAB

Ingredients

250 gms minced meat

3-4 tbsps chana dal

1" piece ginger

6 flakes garlic

4 green chillies

a few coriander leaves

2 cloves

1" cinnamon stick

2 cardamoms

6 peppercorns

1 tsp chilli powder

salt to taste

1 egg

¼ tsp garam masala powder

1 onion

2 green chillies

1 small bunch mint leaves

lime juice

oil to fry

400 gms cream

Method

1. Soak bengal gram for two hours.
2. Boil the keema with the gram, cinnamon, cloves, cardamoms, pepper and a little water till tender.
3. Drain off or dry the excess water.
4. Grind to a paste.
5. Add eggs, salt, chilli powder and ground masala.
6. Cut the onion, green chillies and mint very finely.
7. Mix in salt and lime juice.
8. Add to the keema.
9. Make small flat rounds balls.
10. Fry till brown.
11. After frying put a thin layer of cream in an ovenproof dish.
12. Arrange the kababs over with remaining cream and bake in oven for 15 minutes.
13. Serve with chutney.

28. MEAT BALLS

Ingredients

½ kg mincemeat

2 tbsps garlic-ginger paste

3 green chillies

1 tsp whole spices

1 tsp garam masala

2 tbsps gram flour

1 tsp coriander powder

1 tsps chilli powder

salt to taste

4 tbsps oil for frying

Method

1. Wash the mincemeat.
2. Put in a strainer and gently press to drain out all the water.
3. Put the mince in a bowl.
4. Add all the ingredients. Mix and knead well.
5. Take a pressure pan.
6. Oil its bottom well.
7. Take a heaped tablespoon of mince in the palm of your hand and bind the mince tightly into balls, squeezing out any excess liquid.
8. Make balls a little big as mince tends to shrink after cooking.
9. Add a glassful of water to the oiled pan.
10. Let the water boil well. In the boiling water place the balls gently.

11. After all the balls are put in, let them cook on high flame for 1 minute. Lower the gas to simmer and cook the balls with the pan covered.

12. When the balls are cooked and all the liquid dries up, fry the balls till golden brown.

29. COCONUT FISH FRY

Ingredients

750 gms sole/ bekhti fillets

3 tsps chilli powder

2 tbsps coconut, dessicated

2 tsps ginger, chopped

6 garlic cloves

1½ tbsps white vinegar

3 tsps maida

salt to taste

oil for frying

lemon wedges for garnishing

Method

1. Wash the fish fillets and pat dry.
2. Sprinkle maida over the fillets and keep aside.
3. Grind togeather, chilli powder, coconut, ginger, garlic, vinegar and just enough water to make a fine paste.
4. Add salt and evenly coat the fillets with this paste.
5. Heat oil in a frying pan and fry the fish till crisp.
6. Serve immediately, accompanied by lemon wedges.

30. AMRITSARI MACHCHI

Ingredients

1 kg singhara fish (2" chunks),

deboned and skinned

3 tbsps malt vinegar

2 tbsps ginger paste

2 tbsps garlic paste

½ tbsp chillies (fresh), ground to a paste

1 tsp ajwain (carom seeds)

1 tsp tumeric powder

2 tbsps chilli powder

2 tbsps cumin powder

½ cup eggs, whisked

2 tbsps gramflour

2 tbsps maida

salt to taste

oil for frying

chaat masala to sprinkle on top

Method

1. Wash the fish pieces and pat dry.
2. Dissolve a little salt in vinegar and marinate the fish for 20 minutes.
3. Remove fish from the vinegar, press gently between two paper napkins to remove the moisture.
4. In a bowl, mix the eggs, ginger, garlic and chilli pastes along with the ajwain, turmeric, chilli powder, cumin powder, gramflour, maida, salt and coriander.

5. Evenly coat fish pieces with this mixture and leave to marinate for 30 minutes.
6. Heat the oil in a pan, fry the fish pieces until crisp and golden brown.
7. Drain excess oil, sprinkle chaat masala over them and serve hot, garnished with lemon wedges.

31. CHILLI MUTTON

Ingredients

1 kg mutton

1 cup rajma

4 onions

1 capsicum

6 tomatoes

6 cloves garlic

2 bay leaves

2 tbsps cornflour

2 tsps cumin powder

4 peppercorns

4-5 green chillies

salt and chilli powder to taste

2 tbsps oil

Method

1. Soak the rajma in cold water overnight.
2. Chop the onions and capsicum.
3. Heat the oil in the pan and fry the onions and garlic till brown.
4. Add the capsicum and cook till tender.

5. Add the chilli powder, bay leaf, peppercorn, cumin powder and meat. Brown the mixture and add 5 cups of water and salt to taste.
6. Lower the heat, and let it cook for 45-50 minutes or till done.
7. Meanwhile boil the rajma.
8. When they are done, add them to the meat mixture with the chopped tomatoes.
9. Stir for a while, and then let it cook on low heat for 10–15 minutes.
10. Add the cornflour (mixed with 1 tbsp water) to it and cook till the mixture thickens.
11. Serve hot, garnished with chopped coriander leaves.

CURRIES

CURRIES

1. CHICKEN CHILLI

Ingredients

500 gms boneless chicken

200 gms onion

10 gms ginger

5 big green chillies

1 cup oil

1 tsp soya sauce

2 tsps tomato sauce

1 tsp green chilli sauce

1 small capsicum

a little china salt

1 tbsps vinegar

salt to taste

2 eggs

½ cup cornflour

Method

1. Mix the small chicken pieces with salt, china salt, 1 tsp vinegar and 1 tsp soya sauce.
2. Let them marinate for one hour.
3. Chop the onions and ginger.
4. Slit the capsicum into small pieces and keep it separate.
5. Slit the green chillies in its middle and keep it aside.
6. Break the egg in a small utensil and mix cornflour to it.
7. Add a little water and salt to make a batter.
8. Heat the oil in a or frying pan.
9. Dip the chicken pieces one by one in batter and deep fry it in the oil.
10. Put the green chillies in the oil and then add the onions and fry for a minute till the onions become soft and not red.
11. Then add the mashed and fry for sometime till you get the smell of mixed ginger and onion.
12. Then add the capsicum to it and fry.
13. Then add the chilli sauce and tomato sauce to it.
14. Add the fried chicken and mix thoroughly.
15. Add the salt and let it come to a boil.
16. Serve with mixed fried rice or noodles.

2. CHICKEN CURRY

Ingredients

500 gms chicken, cut into small pieces

1 cup grated coconut

1 medium onion, sliced lengthwise

1 tbsp chopped coriander leaves

1-2 tsp chilli powder

1 tsp coriander powder

¼ tsp turmeric powder

4 cloves

1" cinnamon

7-8 cloves garlic

2" piece ginger

1 medium tomato, chopped

Method

1. Grind all the above ingredients except the chicken, onion and tomato.
2. In a skillet pour 5 tbsps of oil, add the onion and fry till golden brown.
3. Add the tomato and fry until soft, then add the ground masala and fry till the raw smell goes off.
4. Add the chicken, water and salt and bring to a boil.
5. Cook till the chicken is tender and done.
6. Garnish with coriander leaves.

3. CHICKEN HARYALI

Ingredients

1 bunch spinach

2 tsps kasuri methi

2 tbsps curd, beaten

1 kg chicken

2 tbsps oil

salt and pepper to taste

For Wet Spices

a handful of coriander leaves

4 green chillies

5-6 cloves garlic

1 ½ tbsps ginger paste

For Dry Spices

2 ½ tbsps coriander powder

½ tbsp chaat masala

¼ tbsp cinnamon powder

½ tsp clove powder

Method

1. Make a paste of the wet spices and keep aside.
2. Take oil in a skillet and add chicken pieces.
3. Lightly fry them till golden.
4. Add the wet spices and saute for a minute.
5. Add the dry spinach that is coarsely chopped and saute.
6. Add the dry spices and as the spinach wilts saute again lightly.
7. Add the curd and about ½ cup of water.
8. Cover half the skillet and let it cook till the chicken is tender and well cooked.
9. Add salt and pepper.
10. Serve hot.

4. CHICKEN KHOLAPURI

Ingredients

1 kg chicken pieces

1 onion, sliced and browned

1 onion, chopped finely

½ cup chopped tomatoes

1 tsp garlic and ginger paste

1tbsps khus khus

1 tbsp white sesame seeds

4 tbsps coconut dessicated

½ tsp turmeric powder

1 tsp chilli powder

½ tsp garam masala powder

salt to taste

Method

1. Marinate the chicken pieces in garlic, ginger and turmeric powder for half to 1 hour.
2. Dry fry the khus khus, sesame seeds and coconut until brown.
3. Heat a little oil and fry the sliced onions until brown.
4. Grind the browned onions and khus khus mixture and set aside.
5. In a big vessel, heat the oil and add the chopped onions.
6. Fry a while, add ½ tsp each of ginger and garlic paste and fry.
7. Now add the chilli powder and fry.
8. Add the chopped tomatoes and fry until the oil separates.
9. Add the chicken pieces and mix, add a lot of water and allow it to boil.
10. Now add the ground coconut paste, salt and garam masala powder.
11. Cover and cook until done.
12. Serve hot with rice or rotis.

5. EMBASSY CHICKEN

Ingredients

800 gms chicken, cut into 8 pieces

2 tbsps butter

2 onions, chopped finely

8-10 flakes garlic, crushed and chopped

1" ginger piece, chopped finely

2 green chillies chopped finely

2 tbsp maida

2 cups milk

1 ½ cups chicken stock

½ tsps pepper

salt to taste

1 large tomato, chopped finely

2 tbsps tomato ketchup

¼ cup coriander

Method

1. Pressure cook the chicken pieces in 2 cups of water and salt till done.
2. Remove from the fire.
3. When the pressure drops, check to see if the chicken is absolutely tender and soft.
4. Remove the chicken pieces from the stock and keep aside.
5. Reserve the stock and mix with the milk.
6. Heat the butter in a heavy bottom pan.
7. Add onions, garlic, ginger, green chillies.
8. Cook till onions turn transparent.
9. Add the maida.
10. Cook for half a minute.

11. Add the milk and stock mixture to the maida in the pan, stirring continuously for 2 minutes until the sauce thickens.
12. Now add the chicken, tomatoes, pepper and salt.
13. Simmer for a minute.
14. If the sauce gets thick add ½ cup of stock. Boil.
15. Garnish with tomato ketchup and chopped coriander.

6. HYDERABADI CHICKEN

Ingredients

1 chicken, deboned

2 tbsps ginger paste

2 tbsps garlic paste

½ tsp turmeric

1 tbsp chilli powder

½ cup curd

few drops red colour

6-8 curry leaves

5-6 green chillies

2 tbsps cornflour

salt to taste

Method

1. Marinate the chicken with ginger-garlic paste, salt, chilli powder, turmeric and cornflour for a few hours.
2. Heat the oil and fry the chicken pieces on low flame till cooked and well browned.
3. Remove the chicken pieces and keep aside.
4. Mix the colour with the curd.

5. Heat a little oil, add the curry leaves and diced chillies, stir.
6. Add the beaten curd, cook for the few seconds, then add the chicken and cook till all curd dries up and chicken is well coated.
7. Garnish with coriander leaves and lime.

7. JEERA CHICKEN

Ingredients

6 chicken pieces

2 large onions, chopped

2 tsps cumin

2 medium green chillies, chopped

1 tsp soya sauce

1 tsp sesame oil (til oil)

1 tsp garam masala

½ tsp black pepper powder

2 tsps oil

salt to taste

Method

1. Deskin the chicken pieces and keep aside.
2. In a heavy bottom pan fry the onions till brown.
3. When done take out some for garnishing and in the rest add the chicken and stir for 2 minutes.
4. Add the rest of the ingredients and mix well.
5. Cover and cook on low flame till the chicken is done.
6. Place in a serving dish and garnish with fried onions.

8. MASALA CHICKEN

Ingredients

3 potatoes

1 kg chicken, cut into pieces

6 medium onions, chopped

4 medium tomatoes, chopped

6 green chillies, slit

2 tbsps garlic, chopped fine

2 tbsps ginger, chopped

2 peppercorns

8 cloves

6 dry red chillies

2 inch cinnamon stick

oil to cook

salt to taste

Method

1. Peel the potatoes and cut them into long chips /wedges.
2. Heat the oil in a pan.
3. Fry the potato chips /wedges and set aside.
4. Add all the remaining ingredients except chicken to the pan and fry till brown.
5. Then add the chicken pieces and cook till done.
6. Next add fried potato chips /wedges and cook on a slow flame for a few minutes.
7. Serve hot with parathas.

9. ORANGE BAKED CHICKEN

Ingredients

4 boneless, skinless chicken

breasts, halved

2 tbps butter, melted

½ tsp salt

freshly ground pepper

3 tbsps flour

¼ tsp mustard

½ tsp cinnamon

⅛ tsp ground ginger

1½ cups orange juice, boiling

Method

1. Preheat oven to 375°F degrees.
2. Place the chicken breasts in a baking dish.
3. Brush with melted butter sprinkle with salt and pepper.
4. Bake for 15 minutes, uncovered.
5. Put remaining butter in a small saucepan.
6. Add the flour, salt, mustard, cinnamon, and ginger. Cook, stirring for 2 to 3 minutes.
7. Remove from heat and pour on boiling orange juice, beating vigorously with a wire whisk.
8. Cook for 5 minutes, stirring until thickened.
9. Pour over chicken and bake for another 15 minutes.
10. Set oven and brown chicken for 2 to 3 minutes before serving.

10. SHAHI CHICKEN

Ingredients

1 kg chicken (skinless & boneless)

2 tbsps oil

1 large onion, finely chopped.

2 tsps tomato paste

2 tsps poppy seeds powder

2 tsps cashewnut powder

10-15 strands of saffron

2 tbsps milk

1 cup hot water

For Marinating

2 tbsps sp thick curd

2 tbsps coriander powder

2 tbsps cumin powder

1 tbsp ginger paste

1 tsp garlic paste

½ tsp turmeric powder

2 tsps chilli powder

salt

Method

1. Combine all the ingredients for the marinade.
2. Marinate the chicken pieces for 4-5 hours.
3. Heat oil in a vessel and add onions.
4. Stir the fry until onion become light brown in colour.
5. Add the tomato paste, and cashewnut powder, poppy seed powder and fry for 2-3 minutes on a low flame.

6. Add the chicken and mix with the masala.
7. When the chicken will dry add hot water.
8. Cook the chicken on a low flame for 20-25 minutes or till it is well done.
9. Keep stirring occasionally.
10. Melt the saffron in milk and mix with the chicken.
11. Keep on a low flame for 2 minutes.
12. For garnishing sprinkle some chopped coriander leaves and fried onion.

11. TANDOORI CHICKEN

Ingredients

500 gms chicken, skinless, breast, leg and thigh, 2-inch pieces

2 tbsps chilli paste

3 tbsps tandoori paste

2 tbsps Vindaloo paste

2 tbsps curry paste

3 tbsps chilli powder or pepper

4 tbsps yogurt or ½ cup buttermilk

salt to taste

Method

1. Prepare the chicken by removing the skin and trimming off all the fat.
2. Make long slits in the chicken so that the spice mixture can penetrate the meat during marinating.
3. Put all pastes, chilli powder and salt in a bowl.
4. Mix with the paste.

5. Add yogurt (or buttermilk) and mix all the ingredients till you have a smooth paste.
6. Make sure that you do not have any lumps, especially if you use yogurt.
7. Add some water so that all of the chicken will get soaked — do not add too much water to dilute the paste.
8. The paste should have a thick consistency.
9. Soak the chicken in the marinade for 6-8 hours (preferably overnight) in the refrigerator.
10. Heat the oven to 450°F. Prepare a pan for the oven by lining with aluminium foil.
11. Place chicken pieces on the pan and dribble half of the marinade on the pieces.
12. Put the pan in the oven for 15 minutes — uncovered — on middle or top rack.
13. Remove the pan and turn over all of the chicken pieces.
14. Add the remaining marinade on the pieces.
15. Put the pan in the oven for another 15-20 minutes — check to see it is not overcooked.
16. Remove pan and serve the chicken while hot.
17. Garnish with sliced half-rings of onions, green chilli slices and lemon wedges.

12. EGG CAPSICUM

Ingredients

4 eggs

2 capsicums

2 onions

2 green chillies

1 tomato

1 tsp turmeric powder

1 tsp garam masala powder

1 tsp chaat masala

½ tsp black pepper

½ cup oil

salt to taste

Method

1. Boil the eggs and remove their shells.
2. Cut the capsicums into 1½ inch long pieces.
3. Cut the onions and the tomato into long, thick slices.
4. Chop the green chillies finely.
5. Heat a little oil in the pan.
6. Fry the eggs till golden brown and remove them from the pan.
7. Heat some more oil.
8. Add the green chillies, onions and capsicums.
9. Add the vegetables and garam masala, salt, turmeric powder.
10. Fry them till medium tender, then add the sliced tomatoes.
11. Cut the eggs into four long pieces.
12. Sprinkle salt, black pepper and chaat masala over the eggs, adjusting the salt already added to the capsicum.
13. When the capsicum is done, and has blended well with tomatoes and onions, remove from fire.
14. Serve hot with puris or parathas.

13. BOILED EGG KURMA

Ingredients

6 eggs

2 small tomatoes

1 tbsp butter

2 small onions

2 green chillies

1 tsp coriander leaves

½ tsp dry fenugreek leaves

1 tsp tomato ketchup

salt to taste

Method

1. Boil the eggs for 8 to 10 minutes.
2. Remove the yolks from the eggs and cut up the whites into thin slices.
3. Cut the onions and tomatoes into round slices or rings.
4. Heat the butter in a pan, add the onions and fry till they are just transparent.
5. Add slices of tomatoes, green chillies, salt, pepper, coriander leaves, tomato ketchup and egg whites and fry for few minutes.
6. Add the whole egg yolks and fry for a minute more remove.
7. Sprinkle fenugreek leaves on the mixture.

14. SHRIMPS WITH WHITE PUMPKIN

Ingredients

500 gms white pumpkin

1 shrimp

2 tbsps mustard

3 large green chillies

¼ tsp cumin seeds

1 bay leaf

½ tsp coriander powder

½ tsp turmeric powder

½ tsp chilli powder

1 tbsp milk

¼ tsp salt

¼ tsp sugar

Method

1. Peel and cut the pumpkins into very small cubes.
2. Shell, devein and clean the shrimps.
3. Steam along with the pumpkin.
4. Heat the oil and fry the cuminseeds, bay leaf and green chillies for half a minute.
5. Add turmeric, coriander and chilli powder.
6. Fry well for another minute.
7. Add the pumpkin, shrimps, salt, sugar and milk.
8. Cook for 5 minutes till dry.

15. STEAMED PRAWNS

Ingredients

8 medium prawns

1 tbsp turmeric powder

3 dry red chillies

6 green chillies

1 tsp mustard seeds

2 tbsps mustard oil

salt to taste

Method

1. Clean and wash the prawns thoroughly.
2. Add the salt and set aside.
3. Grind the turmeric, red chillies and mustard seeds with a tbsp of water to make a paste.
4. Slit the green chillies.
5. Mix together the prawns, ground paste, oil and green chillies in a double boiler and steam for 15 minutes.
6. Uncover, turn the prawns and steam again for 15 minutes.
7. Serve with boiled rice.

16. PARWAL STUFFED WITH MUTTON

Ingredients

1 kg large, firm parwal

250 gms mutton

1 onion

1" piece ginger

6 cloves garlic

1 tsp garam masala

4 sticks cinnamon

4 cardamoms

4 cloves

½ tsp turmeric powder

½ tsp chilli powder

4 tbsps mustard oil

Method

1. Peel the parwal and make a slit lengthwise in the middle of each; the slit should be large enough for deseeding.
2. Scoop out the seeds from the slit with the help of a narrow scooper.
3. Heat the oil and fry the pawal till brown.
4. Add the minced meat and salt.
5. Fry till done, adding a little water if necessary.
6. When the meat is absolutely dry, remove from the fire and add the garam masala.
7. Stuff the parwal and press the edges of the slit and secure it with a thread.
8. Fry the stuffed parwal lightly in hot oil. Keep aside. In hot oil, add the cardamoms, cloves, cinnamon.
9. Fry for ½ minute.
10. Then add turmeric, chilli powder and salt dissolved in a little water.
11. Fry till the raw smell goes.
12. Add water to the gravy.
13. When it starts boiling lower the heat and add the stuffed parwals.
14. Simmer till done and very little water remains.

17. SPICY EGG CURRY

Ingredients

4 boiled eggs

2 medium-sized onions

1 tomato

3 green chillies

2 tsps coriander powder

5 cloves garlic

1" ginger

1 tsp cumin

½ tsp garam masala

pinch of turmeric powder

3 tbsps oil, water

Method

1. Make a paste of 1 onion, garlic, ginger and green chillies.
2. In a pan heat the oil and add the cumin.
3. When it splutters add the remaining onion (slit lengthwise).
4. Keep frying till it is golden brown and cooked well.
5. Then add finely chopped tomato.
6. Fry till well done.
7. Then add the ground paste, add turmeric powder, coriander powder and salt.
8. Keep frying till you see the oil seperating on the top and there is no raw smell.
9. Add water if the curry sticks on the bottom of the pan.
10. Finally add the boiled eggs (make vertical slits on the sides of the egg).
11. Toss the eggs into the curry and let it simmer for 2 minutes.
12. Sprinkle garam masala and remove from the heat when the curry is thick in consistency.

18. FISH CURRY

Ingredients

1 medium-sized catfish / pomfret

2-3 cloves garlic

1" ginger

handful of coriander leaves

1 tsp coriander, ground

½ cup grated coconut

1 tomato, cut into slices

1 ½ onions, cut, of which cut half of them finely

½ tsp tamarind pulp

2 tsps chilli powder

salt to taste

oil

Method

1. First thaw the fish for about 5-7 minutes.
2. Then wash the fish properly and cut into pieces of 1" each.
3. Add about 2 tsps of turmeric powder and a little salt. Keep aside to marinate for some time.
4. For the gravy grind together the coconut, coriander, coriander seeds, ginger, garlic, tomatoes and one onion.
5. Heat 1-2 tbsps of oil in a pan.
6. To this add the finely cut onion and they fry it till it becomes pinkish in colour.
7. Add a little turmeric powder and chilli powder.
8. To this add the gravy masala.
9. The masala should be added slowly with little water every time of addition, then add the tamarind pulp to it.
10. Stir it constantly.
11. Add the fish pieces to it.

12. Keep it on heat till it boils nicely; keep on stirring.
13. When done garnish with coriander and let it boil again for some time.
14. Enjoy this with steamed rice.

19. MASALA SHRIMP

Ingredients

15 jumbo shrimps

1 big onion, finely diced

1 big onion, cut into chunky pieces,

4 garlic cloves, crushed

1" ginger

2 tomatoes, cut into slices

2 green chillies

1 tsp chilli powder

1 tsp turmeric powder

3 tbsps oil

salt to taste

Method

1. Clean the jumbo shrimps and drain the water.
2. Marinate with half tsp turmeric powder and half tsp salt.
3. Heat 2 tbsps oil in the pan.
4. Add shrimps and deep fry.
5. Remove and transfer into another bowl.
6. Heat 1 tbsp oil in the pan.
7. Add the garlic, ginger, onions and keep frying till they are brown.

8. Add the turmeric powder, cinnamon powder and chilli powder.
9. Stir well. Add the fried shrimp, chunky onion pieces, and fry for a couple of minutes.
10. Add 1 cup water and salt to taste.
11. Let it boil for 4 to 5 minutes.
12. Remove the pan from the flame and garnish the shimps with sliced tomato and green chillies.
13. Serve hot with any main course.

20. PRAWN MALAI CURRY

Ingredients

10-12 medium-sized prawns

2 tbsps bay leaves

2 onion paste

½ tsp ginger paste

1 tsp garlic paste

2 tbsps tomato puree

½ cup coconut milk

1 tbsp ghee

½ tsp turmeric powder

1 tsp chilli powder

salt

½ tsp sugar

½ tsp garam masala powder

coriander leaves

oil

Method

1. Wash and pat dry the prawns.
2. Sprinkle salt and turmeric powder on them.
3. Keep aside.
4. Heat cooking oil in a frying pan.
5. Fry the prawns till light golden.
6. Leave them aside.
7. Add two bay leaves in the remaining oil.
8. Add the onion, ginger and garlic paste carefully into the oil and stir for a minute.
9. Add the tomato puree, turmeric powder, chilli powder, sugar and salt and stir till the oil gets separated from the mixture.
10. Add the prawns now and mix them well.
11. Slowly add the coconut milk and then add half a cup of water.
12. Bring it to boil in low heat.
13. When the curry thickens, spread the ghee and garam masala powder evenly all around the pan.
14. Garnish with coriander leaves.
15. Serve hot with rice or naan.

21. SHRIMP WITH VEGETABLES

Ingredients

½ medium shrimp

few beans

250 gms pumpkin

3 to 4 medium carrots

1 medium potato

3 to 4 small zucchini

2 to 3 flowers broccoli

cabbage

2 medium onions

For the masala

1 tsp panchphoran (a mixture of equal amount of cumin, kalonji, methi, mustard and fennel seeds)

1 tsp turmeric powder

1 tsp chilli powder

salt

a little bit of sugar

cooking oil

Method

1. Heat oil in a heavy bottomed skillet and put the panchphoran in it.
2. Chop the onions finely and fry them with the panchphoran until golden brown.
3. Cut all the vegetables in medium pieces.
4. Clean, devein and wash the shrimps.
5. Fry them with the onions.
6. Add all the vegetables, salt, sugar, turmeric and chilli powder and fry for about five minutes.
7. Cover the skillet with a lid and set the flame to low.
8. Watch that it does not get burnt at the bottom.
9. Sprinkle some water if necessary.
10. Serve hot with rice.

22. ALMOND CHICKEN

Ingredients

300 gms chicken

1 onion

300 gms almonds

1 tomato

300 gms ghee

2 cloves

2 cinnamons

2 cardamoms

2 tsps ginger and garlic paste

3 tsps garam masala powder

4 chillies

3 tsps coriander powder

1 tsp pepper

coriander leaves

mint leaves

Method

1. Heat a pan.
2. Add the ginger and garlic paste, pepper, coriander powder, cloves, cinnamon, almonds cardamom, red chillies.
3. Fry them well.
4. Then grind them finely.
5. Heat 200 gms of ghee in a pan.
6. Add the cut onions and add the tomatoes.
7. After the tomatoes are well fried add the cut chicken, fry them. Add the paste and salt.

8. And let the chicken cook well with the water in the paste and the water from the tomato.
9. Reduce the flame and let the chicken cook for 40 minutes.
10. Add the garam masala and red chillies.
11. Then add the mint leaves and coriander leaves.
12. Finally add the rest of the ghee.
13. Serve hot with rice/chapatis.

Tip : Don't add extra water to cook the chicken, let the chicken cook with the paste. You can also add some lemon at the end to enhance the taste.

23. HOT & SPICY CHICKEN

Ingredients

300 gms chicken

1 onion

1 tomato

2 cloves

2 sticks cinnamon

2 cardamoms

2 tsps ginger & garlic paste

3 tsps garam masala powder

4 tsps chilli powder

8 chillies

200 gms coconut, grated

3 tsps coriander powder

1 tsp pepper

coriander leaves

few mint leaves

Method

1. Heat a pan.
2. Add the cut onions, ginger and garlic paste, coriander powder, cloves, cinnamon, mint leaves cardamom, red chillies and coconut.
3. Fry them well. Then grind them well.
4. Heat 200 gms of oil in a pan, and add the cut onions.
5. Add the tomatoes, and fry well.
6. Add the cut chicken.
7. Fry them for a minute, then add the paste and salt.
8. Let the chicken cook well with the water in the paste and the water from the tomato.
9. Reduce the flame and let the chicken cook for 40 minutes.
10. Add the garam masala and chilli powder.
11. Let the paste simmer well, the oil in the paste should come out separately, the gravy will then taste good.
12. Then add the coriander leaves.
13. Mix well and serve hot with rice/chapatis.

Tip: Don't add extra water to cook the chicken, let the chicken cook with the paste. You can also add some lemon at the end to enhance the taste.

24. PEPPER CHICKEN

Ingredients

2 onions

1 tomato

15 gms ginger

6 tsps pepper

5 tsps coriander powder

2 tsps turmeric powder

curry leaves

coriander leaves

100 gms chicken

Method

1. Cut one onion into big cubes and the other onion into thin strips.
2. Heat some oil in a pan and add the onion cut into big cubes.
3. Fry them until they become golden brown.
4. Then add the coriander powder to the frying mixture.
5. Then finally add the ginger, turmeric powder and pepper to it.
6. Grind them well in the mixer.
7. Heat some oil in a pan.
8. Add the onions and curry leaves cut into strips .
9. When it becomes golden brown, add the tomatoes.
10. When the tomatoes are cooked add the chicken.
11. Reduce the flame and add the paste and salt.
12. Let the paste simmer in the pan with lid on.
13. Cook the chicken for about 45 minutes, but keep stirring every 5 minutes.
14. Finally add the coriander leaves.

Tip : If the masala seems to stick to the bottom add some oil to the masala.

25. MUGHLAI CHICKEN

Ingredients

½ kg chicken

4 chillies

3 tsps ginger paste

3 tsps garlic paste

2 tsps garam masala

1 tsp cuminseeds

6 cloves

6 cardamoms

1 inch cinnamon

1 onion, cut into small pieces

2 potatoes, boiled and peeled

1 tsp turmeric powder

½ cup yogurt, beaten

6 tbsps oil

salt to taste

Method

1. Grind the chillies, cuminseeds, turmeric powder, cloves, cardamom, and cinnamon into a smooth paste.
2. Cut the chicken in the desired size.
3. Apply the ginger and garlic paste, half the ground ingredients, salt and half the yogurt and keep aside for half to 1 hour.
4. Heat some oil in a pan and add the onions until light brown.
5. Add the remaining ground paste and fry.
6. Add the chicken pieces and fry again.
7. Add 2 tsps garam masala powder.
8. Add 1 cup of water and close the vessel so that the chicken can cook.
9. Add the remaining yogurt and the boiled potatoes and let it come to a boil.
10. When the gravy becomes thick, remove from the heat and garnish with coriander leaves.

26. CHICKEN JALFREZI

Ingredients

1 onion, chopped

8 tsps oil

500 gms chicken

4 tsps chilli powder

4 tsps black pepper powder

1 tomato, diced

10 cashewnuts

10 almonds

2 tsps garam masala powder mint leaves

1 tsps turmeric powder corinader leaves

1 capsicum, cut into small pieces

salt to taste

1 potato, boiled and diced

Method

1. Cook the chicken seperately in a vessel of boiling water by adding salt, turmeric powder and 1 tsp of pepper powder.
2. Grind the almonds and cashews.
3. Grind the onions by adding a little water to make into a smooth paste.
4. Heat some oil in a pan and add the onion and nut paste and stir fry for about 2-3 minutes.
5. Add the peppers, diced tomatoes, chilli powder and garam masala powder to it.
6. Add the cooked chicken and boiled potato to it.
7. Continue to stir, add salt to taste.

8. Let it cook for about 7-8 minutes.
9. Then finally add the mint and coriander leaves.
10. Serve hot.

27. MUTTON GRAVY

Ingredients

200 gms mutton

2 tsps ginger-garlic paste

4 cloves

4 sticks cinnamon

4 cardamoms

1 tsp turmeric powder

8 red chillies

5 tsps coconut

1 tsp aniseed (saunf)

2 onions

2 tomatoes

1 tsp coriander powder

coriander leaves

mint leaves

1 tsp garam masala

Method

1. Add a quarter of one onion with the coconut, the spices and red chillies.
2. Grind them well without much water.
3. Heat some oil in a pan.
4. Add the mustard seeds, curry leaves and cut onions.
5. Fry them well till the onions are golden brown.

6. Add the tomatoes, mutton pieces and turmeric powder.
7. Let the mutton cook well for 35 minutes.
8. Add the ground paste and mint leaves, then the coriander powder, salt and garam masala.
9. When the mixture comes to a boil, bring the flame down and let masala simmer for about 20 minutes.
10. Wait until all the water has evaporated.
11. Add the coriander leaves and serve hot with rice.
12. When your gravy is done, the oil will separate from the gravy.

28. MUTTON FRY

Ingredients

300 gms mutton

1 onion, cut

1 tomato

2 cloves

2 sticks cinnamon

2 cardamoms

1 tsps ginger and garlic paste

3 tsps garam masala powder

1 tsp chilli powder

3 tsps chicken masala powder

4 chillies

3 tsps coriander powder

1 tsp pepper

coriander leaves

mint leaves

Method

1. Heat a pan and add the cut onions, ginger-garlic paste, pepper, coriander powder, cloves, cinnamon, cardamom, and chillies.
2. Fry them well. Then grind them finely.
3. Heat 200 gms of oil in a pan, and fry the cut onions.
4. Add the tomatoes, fry well.
5. Add the mutton paste and salt.
6. Let the mutton cook well with the water in the paste and the water from the tomato.
7. Reduce the flame and cook for 40 minutes.
8. Add the garam masala and chicken masala powder, and chilli powder.
9. Then add the mint leaves and coriander leaves.
10. Let the paste simmer and blend with the mutton.
11. It is very important that there should be no extra water.
12. Always cook the mutton on a low flame.
13. Serve hot with rice/chapatis.

29. KASHMIRI GUSTAHA

Ingredients

750 gms lamb, lean (or mutton)

250 gms lamb fat

2 tsps green pepper

2 tsps fennel seeds

1 tsps ginger powder

1 tsp coriander powder

2 tsps kashmiri garam masala

½ cup yoghurt

2 tbsps ghee

1 tsps sugar

½ cup khoya

1 cup milk

2 tsps pepper

4 cardamoms

Method

1. Chop the meat, and add green pepper, fennel, ginger, coriander, and 1 tsp garam masala in a food processor.
2. Keep the mixie running, adding a little yogurt and ghee, until the meat is a smooth paste.
3. Form into balls 1.5-2 inches in diameter.
4. Heat the remaining ghee in a pan.
5. Add the sugar, khoya, yogurt, garam masala, and salt to taste.
6. Pour in the milk, add the koftas, and simmer until the liquid evaporates and the koftas are very tender.

30. BOMBAY SHRIMP

Ingredients

½ kg medium-size shrimps

1 tsp garlic paste

1 tsp ginger paste

4 tsps tamarind paste

¼ tsp turmeric powder

¼ tsp chilli powder

salt to taste

2 tbsps vegetable oil

3 cloves garlic

½ cup coconut milk

½ tbsp finely chopped coriander

2 finely green chillies chopped

Method

1. Devein the shrimps.
2. Put them in a pot.
3. Add the garlic, ginger, tamarind paste, turmeric, salt and chilli powder.
4. Mix well and keep aside for 10 minutes.
5. Heat the oil in a frying pan.
6. Add whole cloves of garlic.
7. Stir until brown.
8. Add the shrimps and stir for a minute so that the shrimps also get brown.
9. Add the coconut milk, coriander and green chillies.
10. Turn the heat off as the gravy begins to simmer.
11. Serve on a bed of steamed rice.

31. CRAB CURRY

Ingredients

4 whole crabs

2 big potatoes

2 onions

2 cloves

2 cardamoms

½ stick cinnamon

3" ginger

5 cloves garlic

8 red chillies

1 medium-sized tomato

2 tsps cumin powder

2 tsps coriander powder

2 tsps salt

1 tsp sugar

Method

1. Clean the crabs.
2. Make a fine paste with ginger, garlic and red chillies.
3. Chop the onions fine.
4. Peel and chop the potatoes.
5. Heat the oil.
6. Add the cardamom, cloves and cinnamon and fry for a minute.
7. Add the crabs and fry them well.
8. When fried, take them out and put them aside.
9. This should take 3-4 minutes of frying at high temperature, at the most 5 minutes.
10. Fry the potatoes for 2 minutes.
11. Add the minced onions.
12. Fry till the onions are well done.
13. Add the ginger and garlic paste.
14. Now add the chopped tomatoes, cumin and coriander powder, salt and sugar.

15. Fry until the oil seperates.
16. Put the crabs back in and mix well.
17. Add water enough to drown the crabs, and boil for 15 minutes.
18. Serve hot.

32. MOGLI CHOPS

Ingredients

4 mutton chops

1 onion

2 garlic flakes

1" ginger

300 ml curd

1 tbsp coriander leaves

2 tsps chilli powder

2 tsps garam masala

60 ml oil

1 tsp salt

Method

1. Chop the onion and garlic.
2. Cut the ginger into strips.
3. Blend the onion, garlic and ginger with the curd, coriander leaves and remaining spices in a blender to get a smooth paste.
4. With a fork prick the chops all over.
5. Pour the marinade over the chops and leave for 8 hours or overnight.
6. Next day heat the oil in a frying pan and fry the chops with the marinade until they are cooked.
7. Cook the chops on a low flame so that the chops cook thoroughly.

33. SWEET & SOUR CHICKEN

Ingredients

170 gms boneless and skinless

5 cups chicken stock chicken

1 tbsp light soya sauce

10 tsps all purpose flour

1½ tbsps vinegar

1 tbsp sugar

1 tbsp tomato paste

1 tsp cornflour

1 tsp water

4 small pieces of pineapple

salt

Method

1. Combine the chicken stock, soya sauce, salt, vinegar, sugar and tomato paste in a large saucepan.
2. Bring to the boil and add the pineapple pieces.
3. Blend together cornflour and water and add to the sauce.
4. Simmer. Mix the sauce with 10 tsps all-purpose flour and the chicken.
5. Marinate the chicken for about 20 minutes.
6. Deep fry them in oil till the chicken becomes golden brown.

34. AKHINI

Ingredients For Akhini

1 kg mutton

¾ kg basmati rice

8 big onions

25 green chillies

50 gms ginger

1 tsp big jeera

1 tsp cumin

4 cardamoms

6 cloves

2 pieces cinnamon

3 tomatoes

1 ½ cups curd

2 limes

2 tsps chopped coriander leaves

oil

salt to taste

For the Chutney

100 gms small onions, chopped

3 green chillies

1" ginger

few curry leaves

few coriander leaves

1 tsp chilli powder

2 tsps sugar

thick tamarind water

salt to taste

Method

1. Heat the oil.
2. Add the garam masala, onion and green chillies.
3. Fry lightly and add the other masalas except lime and coriander leaves.

4. Add the mutton with it and keep it in cooker for 15 minutes.
5. Fry rice in oil for 3 to 4 minutes and add all the ingredients.
6. Add 3 to 4 cups of water.
7. Keep on high pressure for 5 to 7 minutes and lower the pressure and cook for 10 minutes.
8. For the chutney grind all the ingredients well.
9. Serve Akhini with the chutney.

35. METHI MUTTON

Ingredients

½ kg mutton chops

1 cup curd, well beaten

¾ cup coriander leaves

½ cup methi leaves

2 potatoes

1 tomato

8 peppercorns

4 Kashmiri chillies

3-4 green chillies

3 cloves

2 cardamoms

2 sprigs mint leaves

1 big stick cinnamon

5 tsps coriander seeds

1 tsp cumminseeds

1 tsp poppy seeds

1 tsp ginger-garlic paste

1 tsp dried methi leaves, crushed

salt

ghee for frying

Method

1. Roast the peppercorns, cardamoms, cloves, cinnamon, poppy seeds, coriander seeds, cuminseeds and red chillies and grind to a fine powder.
2. Fry the green chillies and onions with a little ghee and grind them along with the coriander leaves, mint leaves and powdered spices, to a fine paste.
3. Heat ghee in a pan.
4. Add the mutton pieces and fry for a minute.
5. Add the methi leaves and salt and fry for three minutes.
6. Pour the ground masala paste over the chops and fry for five minutes, adding just half a cup of water.
7. Add the curds and mix well.
8. Just before covering the pan, add the tomato and potato pieces.
9. Cook till the mutton is done.
10. Uncover the pan and add the dry methi leaves.
11. Simmer for a few minutes.
12. Serve hot with the remaining coriander leaves.

36. MUTTON VEGETABLE MASALA

Ingredients

1 kg boneless mutton (or chicken), boiled and shredded

200 gms french beans, chopped

100 gms carrots, cut into medium-sized pieces

200 gms green peas

2 big potatoes, boiled and cut into pieces

½ bunch mint leaves

2 tbsps maida

whole garam masala, according to taste

1 garlic, skinned and crushed

1 tbsp ghee

1 cup milk

1 tsp each of ginger, garlic and green chilli paste

2 eggs, hard boiled

salt to taste

1 tomato

Method

1. Add the masala paste and salt in mutton and pressure cook with sufficient water until done.
2. Shred the mutton and keep aside.
3. Boil the vegetables with 1 tsp salt.
4. Preserve a little of the water.
5. Heat ghee in a heavy bottom pot.
6. Add the garam masala and fry till it crackles.
7. Then add the crushed garlic and fry till it is golden brown.
8. Add the maida and fry for two minutes.
9. Add the preserved water (mutton) a little at a time and keep stirring so that no lumps are formed.
10. Add the preserved water (vegetable) and stir.
11. Add the shredded mutton and vegetables and bring to a boil.
12. Then add the milk till the gravy thickens.
13. Serve hot, garnished with mint leaves and sliced eggs.

37. SPICY MUTTON

Ingredients

¾ kg mutton

2 onions

6 green chillies

curry leaves

4 tsps ginger-garlic paste

1 tomato

1 ½ tsps garam masala

1 ½ tsps coriander powder

Method

1. Marinate the mutton with ½ tsp chilli powder and sufficient salt for 1-2 hours.
2. Fry the chopped onions, chilles, curry leaves, and ginger-garlic paste. After a few the minutes, and the garma masala.
3. When the onions are cooked, add the coriander powder, chilli powder and a pinch of turmeric.
4. Mix well.
5. Add tomato and fry for 2 minutes.
6. Put the mutton with masala in the cooker and add some water.
7. Pressure cook for 10 minutes (at least).
8. To make the gravy, add the coconut milk and let the meat simmer in it for a few minutes.
9. Serve hot with plain rice.

38. SHIKAMPUR KOFTA

Ingredients

1 kg mutton

2 tsps khuskhus

1 tsp chironji

2 tsps garam masala powder

1 tsp chilli powder

salt

1 egg

1 big onion

coriander leaves, chopped

mint

2 green chillies

2 cups yogurt

oil

Method

1. Boil the keema with a pinch of turmeric powder and salt.
2. Roast the khuskhus, coriander, mint, green chillies and grind them.
3. After the keema is well cooked add it to the ground mixture.
4. Add the garam masala powder, chilli powder and egg and mix well.
5. Put yogurt in a muslin cloth.
6. Add salt, green chillies, coriander, onion, mint, and tie the end of the cloth.
7. Keep aside till all the water oozes out from the yogurt and becomes dry.

8. Now take the keema mixture and fill it with the yogurt mixture; flatten them on the pan and shallow fry them.
9. Garnish with onion and coriander.

39. PASINDE

Ingredients

500 gms boneless mutton

¾ cup curd, beaten

1 tsp chilli powder

¼ tsp turmeric

2 tsps khuskhus

10 almonds

2 tsps garam masala

2 tsp ginger-garlic paste

2 onions, fried

2 tsps coriander powder

4 tsp oil

coriander and mint leaves

salt

Method

1. To the mutton apply the ginger-garlic paste, curd and salt and keep aside.
2. Lightly roast and powder the khuskhus and almond.
3. Heat the ghee and fry the onions.
4. Remove half of it and keep aside for garnishing.
5. To the remaining half of the fried onions add the mixed mutton, chilli powder, turmeric and fry till dry.

6. Add the powdered masala and garam masala and fry a little.
7. Then add two cups of water and cook till the mutton is tender.
8. Finally sprinkle the remaining fried onion, chopped coriander and mint.
9. Serve with rice and dal.

40. BRINJAL PRAWN CURRY

Ingredients

250 gms prawns, medium side

100 gms brinjal, cut into large slices

100 gms tomatoes, chopped

½ tbsp cumin

½ tbsp mustard

½ tbsp turmeric

4 cloves garlic a

¼ ginger.

paste with 2 tbsps of water

5 tbsps of oil

½ cup of water

Method

1. Clean the prawns.
2. Grind together 1 tbsp cumin, mustard , 3 green chillies and coriander leaves to a fine paste.
3. Heat 2 tbsps of oil in a frying pan, and fry the brinjal until golden brown.
4. Keep aside. Then fry the prawns on low heat until golden brown.

5. Keep aside. Heat the remain oil, then add the tbsp of cumin and mustard.
6. Then add the chopped tomato and cook for 2 to 5 minutes.
7. Add the fried prawns first and stir well.
8. Add the brinjal paste and turmeric and salt to taste and let it cook for 5 minutes.
9. Add a cup of water. Keep your pan in high heat up to boiling point, then reduce the heat and keep it on low to medium heat for 5 minutes.
10. Serve hot with rice.

41. CHICKEN HAZAARVI

Ingredients

8 pieces chicken breasts (boneless)

2 tsps ginger paste

2 tsps garlic paste

1 tsp white pepper powder

salt as per taste

½ cup cheese, grated

4 green chillies

¼ tsp mace powder

¼ tsp nutmeg powder

2 tsps chopped coriander leaves

1 egg

¾ cup fresh cream

butter for basting

Method

1. Cut the chicken breasts into two-inch cubes.
2. Apply the ginger paste, garlic paste, white pepper powder and salt to the chicken cubes and keep aside.
3. Mash the cheese to make it into a smooth paste.
4. Add finely chopped green chillies, mace powder, nutmeg powder, coriander leaves and salt.
5. Add the egg and mix well.
6. Add the chicken to the cheese mixture.
7. Then add fresh cream and mix gently.
8. Keep in the refrigerator for about two to three hours.
9. Put the chicken onto the skewers and cook in a moderately hot tandoor or a pre-heated oven (200 degrees Celsius) until it is just cooked and slightly coloured.
10. Apply a little butter for basting and cook for another two minutes till the chicken is fully cooked.

42. BUTTER CHICKEN

Ingredients

1 tandoori chicken, cut into 8 pieces

1 onion, grated

1 tsp ginger paste

1 tsp garlic paste

¾ cup tomato puree

½ tsp chilli powder

2-3 green chillies, finely chopped

100 gms butter

salt to taste

200 gms cream

a few green coriander leaves, finely chopped

Method

1. Melt butter in a frying pan. Add the grated onions and fry until golden brown.
2. Add the ginger and garlic paste.
3. Fry for a minute and add the tomato puree.
4. Add the chopped green chillies, coriander leaves, salt and the chilli powder.
5. Fry for 2-3 minutes.
6. Turn the heat to low and add the cream, stirring constantly.
7. Do not let it boil.
8. Cook for a minute and turn off the heat.
9. Arrange tandoori chicken pieces in an ovenproff dish.
10. Pour the sauce on it.
11. Heat in a rejeated oven at 180° C/350° F for 20 minutes .
12. Serve hot.

43. MASAALEDAR MACHCHI

Ingredients

750 gms bekdi / singhara fish

(boneless), cut into small fillets

3 tbsps oil

1onion, finely chopped

1½ tsps kalonji (onion seeds)

6 dry red chillies

2 tsps garlic, finely chopped

2 tomatoes, chopped

3 tbsps coconut, desiccated

salt to taste

1½ tsps coriander powder

1½ tsps cumin powder

1 tsp chilli powder

½ cup water

2 tbsps lemon juice

2 tbsps coriander leaves, finely chopped

Method

1. Wash and pat dry the fish.
2. Heat oil in a frying pan.
3. Add the onions and fry until soft.
4. Add the kalonji, and garlic, cook for 2-3 minutes.
5. Add the tomatoes, coconut, salt, coriander, cumin and chilli powders.
6. Cook for 10 minutes.
7. Add the fish pieces along with water.
8. Cook for 10 minutes, until the fish is tender and water has almost evaporated.
9. Mix in the lemon juice and coriander leaves.
10. Serve hot with Jeera Pulao.

44. MALAI MEAT

Ingredients

750 gms boneless mutton, cut into 1" inch cubes

2 tbsps lemon juice

½ cup thick curd

3 tbsps thick cream

½ tbsp nutmeg powder

1 nutmeg

½ tbsp green cardamom powder

1 ½ tsps ginger paste

1 ½ tsps garlic paste

1 tsp garam masala

½ cup finely chopped coriander leaves

1 tbsp oil

2 onions, finely sliced

1 tsp cuminseeds

salt to taste

Method

1. Mix the boneless mutton cubes with the lemon juice and salt and leave aside for 2 hours.
2. Mix them with ginger paste, garlic paste, curd, cream, nutmeg powder, cardamom powder and salt.
3. Leave to marinate overnight.
4. Heat oil in a heavy bottomed pan and add the cuminseeds.
5. When they splutter, add the mutton with the marinate.

6. Cover and simmer until just tender.
7. Add the sliced onions, garam masala and fresh coriander leaves.
8. Cook for 10-15 minutes on a medium flame.
9. Serve hot with parathas.

45. CHICKEN KANDHARI KOFTA

Ingredients

500 gms chicken mince

½ tsp cinnamon powder

salt to taste

3 tsps oil

¾ cup boiled onion paste

1 tsp ginger-garlic paste

1 tsp coriander powder

1 tsp chilli powder

½ cup tomato puree

¼ cup cashewnut paste

½ tsp garam masala powder

2 tbsps pomegranate syrup

½ cup fresh cream

Method

1. Mix the cinnamon powder, one teaspoonful of salt and minced chicken thoroughly.
2. Divide the mix into twelve equal portions.
3. Shape them into koftas. Keep aside.
4. Heat oil in a pan.
5. Add the boiled onion paste and cook till onion turns pink.
6. Add the ginger-garlic paste.

7. Saute for a minute, then add coriander powder and chilli powder.
8. Stir in the tomato pure and cashewnut paste dissolved in a little water.
9. Cook for five minutes on a high flame, stirring continuously.
10. Add one and half cups of water and bring it to a boil.
11. Add the chicken koftas and cook for ten minutes, stirring occasionally. 12. Add the garam masala powder and pomegranate syrup.
13. Simmer for five minutes.
14. Stir in fresh cream.
15. Serve with naan or paratha.

46. CHICKEN DO PYAZA

Ingredients

1 ½ kg chicken (whole)

4 onions, thinly sliced

3 cups tomato puree

1 tbsp finely chopped garlic

2 tbsp finely chopped ginger

1 tbsp finely chopped green chilli

1 tsp chilli powder

2 tsps garam masala powder

1 tsp coriander powder

½ tsp turmeric powder

salt to taste

7 tbsp vegetable oil

chopped coriander leaves for garnishing

Method

1. Thoroughly clean the chicken and cut into pieces.
2. Heat oil in a pan.
3. Add the ginger, garlic and green chilli and fry over medium heat for 2 minutes.
4. Add the tomato puree, garam masala, turmeric powder, chilli powder, coriander powder and salt.
5. Bring it to boil and then cook on medium for 5 minutes.
6. Add the sliced onions and cook until it becomes tender.
7. Add the chicken pieces.
8. Stir well so that all the chicken pieces are coated well with gravy.
9. Add water.
10. Bring it to boil on high and then reduce the heat to medium.
11. Cover the pan and cook until the chicken is tender and the gravy becomes thick.
12. Garnish with coriander leaves and serve hot.

47. KADAI CHICKEN

Ingredients

1 whole chicken

3-4 onions, chopped

6-7 tomatoes, chopped

2 tsps ginger paste

2 tsps garlic paste

3 green chillies, chopped

2 tsps coriander powder

2 tsps garam masala powder

1½ tsps chilli, powder

½ tsp turmeric powder

salt to taste

vegetable oil as required

coriander leaves for garnishing

Method

1. Thoroughly clean the chicken and cut into pieces.
2. Heat oil in a kadai.
3. Add the chopped onions and green chilli and fry until light golden brown in colour.
4. Add the chilli powder, turmeric powder, garam masala, coriander powder and salt. Mix well.
5. Add the tomatoes, ginger, garlic paste and cook until the tomatoes become tender.
6. Add a little water and bring it to a boil.
7. When the gravy becomes slightly thick, cook for 10-15 minutes (or until fully cooked). If you have a copper-based kadai then transfer the contents into it.
8. Heat for a while.
9. Then garnish with coriander leaves and serve hot.

48. PALAK CHICKEN

Ingredients

½ kg chicken

1 bunch spinach

3 onions

12 cloves garlic

6-8 green chillies

coriander leaves, finely chopped

4 cloves

1 stick cinnamon

1 bay leaf

½ cup yogurt

oil for frying

salt to taste

Method

1. Finely chop the onions, garlic and green chillies.
2. Boil the spinach on low heat in a vessel till it is soft.
3. Switch off and set aside.
4. Heat oil in a wok/pan.
5. Add the cloves, cinnamon, and bay leaf.
6. Fry for a minute.
7. Add the onions till they turn pink.
8. Add the finely chopped garlic, green chillies and coriander.
9. Add the spinach to this mixture.
10. Fry this mixture for a couple of minutes.
11. Take the mixture off the heat.
12. Use the blender to grind the spinach mixture to a paste.
13. Heat some more oil in pan.
14. Add the paste from the blender.
15. Add the curd once the oil starts leaving the sides of the pan.
16. Add the chicken and salt.
17. Cook on low heat till the chicken is done.
18. Serve with hot rotis or rice.

49. MUTTON IN CURD AND GREEN CHILLIES

Ingredients

1 kg mutton

250 gms potatoes, cut into big pieces

250 gms curd

125 gms onions

2" piece ginger

10 cloves garlic

2 tsps coriander powder

8 green chillies

125 gms ghee

3 sticks cinnamon

8 cardamoms

8 cloves

salt to taste

Method

1. Marinate the mutton pieces with the ground paste, salt and curd for an hour.
2. Heat the ghee and add the cinnamon, cardamoms and cloves.
3. Add the mutton and simmer on a low fire.
4. When the meat becomes tender, add the green chillies and potatoes.
5. Cook till the potatoes are done and the gravy becomes thick.

RICE AND NOODLES

RICE AND NOODLES

1. AMERICAN CHOPSUEY

Ingredients

1 can tomato juice

1 tbsp salt

4 tbsps vinegar

4-5 tbsps sugar

4 tbsps cornflour

1 cup water

1 cup broccoli florets

½ cup sliced beans

½ cup bean sprouts

½ cup chopped cabbage

½ cup chopped capsicum

½ cup carrots cut into julienes

2 packets of crisp fried noodles

3-4 eggs

oil for stir frying

Method

1. Combine the juice, vinegar, cornflour, salt, sugar and water in a blender.
2. Then boil in a saucepan on a low heat stirring continuously till you obtain a medium thick sauce.
3. Keep aside. In a pan add 1-2 tablespoon of oil.
4. Heat on high flame.
5. Add all the veggies except capsicum and cabbage.
6. Stir-fry till somewhat tender.
7. Do not overcook.
8. The add the cabbage and capsicum.
9. Stir-fry for a few more minutes.
10. Take off from heat. Keep aside.
11. Quickly mix the sauce prepared above with the veggies prepared.
12. Heat gently.
13. Do not boil.
14. In a non-stick pan fry the eggs individually in a little oil and keep aside.
15. Put a handful of fried noodles in a plate.
16. Heap a lot of veggie-sauce mixture over the noodles.
17. Top with a fried egg.
18. Serve immediately with chopped green chillies and soya sauce.

2. BAKED PISTACHIO RICE

Ingredients

250 gms rice cooked in salt water

50 gms pistachio paste

1 cup chicken, boiled and shredded

2-3 tbsps butter

2 cups spring onions, chopped

1 tbsp flour

1 cup milk

½ cup chicken stock

3-4 chillies, chopped

salt and pepper to taste

½ tsp ajinomoto

carrots for garnishing

few pistachios, chopped

Method

1. Heat the butter and saute 1 cup onions.
2. Add the chicken and cook for 2 minutes.
3. Add the flour, saute till light brown.
4. Add the pistachio paste, saute for 1 minute. Gradually add the milk, stock, chillies and half a cup of spring onion.
5. Cook for 2-3 minutes.
6. Then season with salt, pepper and ajinomoto and remove from the fire.
7. Fry the remaining spring onions in oil, add the rice and remove from the fire.
8. Grease an ovenproof dish, spread half the rice, spread the sauce over it and cover with the remaining rice.
9. Sprinkle some chopped pistachio on the rice and knobs of butter.
10. Bake for 10 minutes.
11. Decorate with chopped carrot.

3. CHICKEN BIRYANI

Ingredients For Marinating

4 cloves

3 sticks cinnamon

2 cardamoms

½ kg chicken

2 tbsps curd

1 tsp turmeric powder

3 tsps chilli powder

1 tsp tandoori masala powder

salt to taste

3 cups basmati rice

For Grinding

4 onions

10 green chillies

12 cloves garlic

1" ginger

3 tomatoes

Method

1. Marinate the meat in the marinating ingredients and keep aside.
2. Refregerate for about an hour to 90 minutes.
3. Heat the vegetable shortening or oil (3 tbsps) in a pan.
4. Add the cloves , cinnamon cardamoms, and fry well .
5. Add the ground paste and fry till the oil comes up.
6. Add the marinated chicken and fry.
7. Cover for some time.

8. Then add the rice and fry.
9. Add the coriander and mint leaves and cook in the rice cooker.
10. Add water just enough to submerge the rice and chicken.
11. Close the pan and cook on a low flame till the rice is cooked.
12. Serve with onion raita.

4. EGG BIRYANI

Ingredients

2 cups basmati rice washed and soaked for 10 minutes

6 large eggs

1 onion, sliced thin

10 green chillies, slit

1 bay leaf

4 cloves

½ tsp peppercorns

1 inch cinnamon

1 tsp each of ginger and garlicpaste

1 tsp pulao masala

salt to taste

2 tbsp oil

Method

1. Hard boil 4 eggs and remove their shells.
2. Heat oil in a large dish and add the whole spices
3. After a few seconds add the onion and green chillies along with the ginger-garlic paste.
4. Fry till light brown.
5. Now break the remaining two eggs into the pan and scramble.

6. Add the drained rice to it and fry for a minute.
7. Add salt.
8. Now put the boiled eggs into it and pour 4 cups of water.
9. Cover and cook till the rice is half done.
10. Stir in the pulao masala and a little bit of lemon juice and mix gently.
11. Cover and cook till all the water evaporates and the rice is done.
12. Garnish with coriander.
13. Serve hot.

5. EGG NOODLES

Ingredients

1 packet plain noodles

1 onion, cut into small pieces

2 tbsps tomato juice

1 tsp ginger and garlic paste

½ tsp garam masala

1 tsp chilli powder

1 tsp pepper powder

1egg

1 tbsp oil

salt as required

Method

1. Take 500 ml water in a vessel and allow it to boil.
2. When boiling add the noodles and cook for 3 minutes.
3. Drain the water and keep the cooked noodles separately.
4. Heat the oil in a pan and fry the onion till it becomes golden brown.
5. Add the ginger and garlic paste, chilli powder, pepper powder, garam masala powder and fry for 2 minutes.

6. Then break the egg into it and fry well.
7. Add the tomato juice into it and cook for 1 minute.
8. Add the salt and mix these with the cooked noodles

6. MINT AND EGG FRIED RICE

Ingredients

2 cups bolied rice

1 bunch mint leaves, ground to a paste

2 eggs

fresh chopped coriander

5 green tomatoes, cut in long thin pieces

1 big onion, cut in long, thin pieces

1 tsp green chilli paste

salt

½ tsp mustard seeds

½ tsp cumin

½ tsp ground black pepper

curry leaves

5 to 6 tsps vegetable oil

Method

1. Heat a pan on medium heat, Add the oil and mustard seeds.
2. When the mustard splutters add the cumin, ground pepper, curry leaves and fry them for 1 minute.
3. Add the cut onion, fry for a minute.
4. Add the cut tomato, fry for 2 minutes.
5. Add the green chilli paste, mint paste and eggs.
6. Crack the eggs into the pan and beat them until it mixes well with the tomato and onion pieces.

7. Fry for 2 minutes.
8. Meanwhile boil the rice in a rice cooker.
9. Mix the boiled rice with the above mixture and fry for 4 to 5 minutes.
10. Garnish with chopped coriander.

7. GREEN PRAWN PULAO

Ingredients

1 cup basmati rice, washed and drained.

1 cup shelled, deveined prawns

1 tsp turmeric powder

½ tsp shahjeera

½ cup chopped coriander leaves

oil for frying

salt to taste

For the Ground Masala

3-4 green chillies

2 tsps chopped garlic.

7-8 peppercorns

5-6 cloves

1 tsp chopped ginger

1 inch cinnamon

Method

1. Wash the prawns, apply the salt and turmeric powder and leave aside for 15 minutes.
2. Shallow fry the prawns in oil but do not let them harden.

3. Heat 2 tbsps oil, add the shahjeera.
4. When they splutter add the ground masala and fry till the oil separates.
5. Then add the drained rice and fry for 2 minutes.
6. Add one and a half cups water to it, add salt and mix well.
7. When the water boils reduce the flame and cook the rice on a slow fire till done.
8. Fluff up the rice with a fork and mix the fried prawns.
9. Sprinkle some of the oil used for frying prawns on the rice.
10. Cover and leave on slow fire for five minutes.
11. Serve with salad, pickle and omelette.

8. PRAWN PULAO

Ingredients

½ cup prawns

3 tsps ginger-garlic paste

5 green chillies

1 tsp jeera powder

1 onion

5 tomatoes

½ cup grated coconut

½ cup coconut milk

¼ cup oil

salt-according to taste

2 ½ cups basmati rice

7 or 8 cloves

3 tsps cinnamon powder

3 cardamoms

salt

3 tsps butter

Method

1. Add water and parboil the rice.
2. Drain and keep aside.
3. Put the pan on fire, add half of the oil. Add thinly sliced onions and then fry until golden brown.
4. Remove and keep aside.
5. Now add the ginger-garlic paste, green chilli paste and fry until a nice aroma comes.
6. Then add the cleaned prawns and fry for 3-4 minutes.
7. Then add the cumin powder, cut tomatoes and mix well. Cook on a medium heat until they soften.
8. Now add the grated coconut, coconut milk, salt and garam masala powder.
9. Remove after 5 minutes.
10. Empty the gravy into a casserole and top it with parboiled rice.
11. Garnish with fried onions, finely cut coriander and a few mint leaves.
12. Cover with a lid, seal the sides with atta dough and cook on slow heat till rice is done.
13. Serve hot with raita.

9. CHICKEN BIRIYANI

Ingredients

4 cups basmati rice, soaked for ½ hour

1tbsp ginger paste

1 tbsp garlic paste

6 green chillies

1 onion finely,chopped

2 tomatoes, finely chopped

10 gms each cinnamon, cloves, cardamom

100 gms cashewnuts

200 gms ghee

150 gms chicken

2 tsps garam masala powder

3 tsps chilli powder

mint and coriander leaves

½ tsp lemon

Method

1. In hot ghee fry the onions and tomatoes.
2. Add the cashewnuts, cloves, cinnamon, and cardamom.
3. Add the mint leaves, coriander leaves, green chillies, ginger and garlic pastes.
4. Stir-fry and then add the garam masala, chilli powder and chicken to it.
5. Add 1cup water and salt to taste.
6. Bring the mixture to a boil and add the rice.
7. Add the lemon juice to it and then let the rice be cooked.
8. Serve hot.

10. MINT CHICKEN BIRIYANI

Ingredients

4 cups basmati rice, soaked for ½ hour

1 tbsp ginger-garlic paste

6 green chillies

1 onion, finely chopped

2 tomatoes, finely chopped

10 gms each cinnamon, cloves, cardamom

4 cups thick coconut milk

100 gms cashewnuts

200 gms ghee

100 gms chicken

2 tsps garam masala powder

3 tsps chilli powder

mint and coriander leaves

½ tsps lemon juice

Method

1. Dilute the coconut milk, in the ratio of 1 cup of rice to 2 cups of diluted coconut milk.
2. Add ghee to a pan.
3. Fry the onions and tomatoes.
4. Grind the cashewnuts, cloves, cinamon, cardamom, green chillies, mint and coriander leaves.
5. Add the mixture to the ghee.
6. Saute for a minute.
7. Add the ginger-garlic paste.
8. Then add the garam masala, chilli powder and chicken to it.
9. Saute for a minute.
10. Add the coconut milk, and salt to taste.
11. Bring the mixture to a boil and add the rice.
12. Add the lemon juice to it and then let the rice be cooked.
13. Serve hot.

11. MIXED CHICKEN PULAO

Ingredients

1 chicken, medium

2 cups basmati rice

6 cups water

1 bay leaf

2 sprigs parsley

2 spring onions

1 cup prawns, boiled

1 cup crabmeat, sliced

1 cup ham, sliced

1 tsp cuminseeds, powdered

1 tsp coriander seeds, powdered

1 tsp garam masala powder

salt and chilli powder to taste

4 tsps groundnuts, roasted and ground

Method

1. Place the chicken in a pan filled with 6 cups water.
2. Add the spring onions, bay leaf, parsley, salt, and all the spices.
3. Cook till the chicken is tender.
4. Strain the stock. It should be about 4 cups; if it is less, add water to make up the quantity.
5. Remove all the meat from the bones of the ham and cut into strips.
6. Combine the stock and rice and cook with ham till the rice is tender and dry.
7. Mix in the rest of the above ingredients and serve hot.

12. DUM BIRIYANI

Ingredients

1½ cups basmati rice

1 kg chicken

2 medium sized onions, finely

3 medium sized tomatoes, finely sliced

5 potatoes

2 tsps ginger-garlic paste

3-4 green chillies

2 tsps mint leaves

2 tsps coriander leaves, roughly chopped

6 tsps ghee

2 green cardamom

3 cinnamons

3 black cardamoms

3 bay leaves

3 cloves

4-5 saffron strands

3 tsps warm milk

½ tsp turmeric powder

1 tsp chilli and coriander powder

1½ cups yogurt

salt as per taste

4 cups water

Method

1. Clean the chicken.
2. Cut into half-inch sized pieces.

3. Clean, wash and soak the rice in the water.
4. Soak the saffron in warm milk and keep aside.
5. Marinate the chicken pieces with turmeric, salt, yogurt,1 tbsp of ginger-garlic pastes for 4 hours in a cool place.
6. Now cook the rice in salted boiling water along with cardamoms, cinnamons, cloves and bay leaves.
7. Rice should be half cooked; retain the strained water.
8. Keep the rice warm.
9. Heat ghee in a pan or pressure cooker.
10. Add the sliced onions and green chillies.
11. Cook until golden brown, make sure to stir continuously.
12. Add the remaining ginger-garlic paste, mix well.
13. Now add the marinated chicken pieces and cook on high flame stirring continuously for 7-8 minutes.
14. Add the coriander and chilli powder and mix thoroughly.
15. Stir in 3 cups of water, bring to boil, reduce heat and cook covered till the chicken pieces are almost cooked.
16. Add the tomatoes and potatoes, half a tsp of garam masala powder, half the chopped mint and coriander leaves.
17. Cook for 15 minutes on medium heat, stirring occasionally.
18. In case you are cooking in the pressure cooker it normally takes 2 whistles.
19. Ensure that the cooked chicken does not have a runny gravy.
20. If it is so cook on high flame and reduce the water content.
21. Take a cooker, mix the warm rice and chicken masala, check the salt.
22. Sprinkle the remaining mint-coriander leaves, saffron milk and 2 tbsp of ghee.

23. In the end sprinkle a glass of retained water.
24. Cover it with a moist cloth and seal it with a lid.
25. Cook it for 15-20 minutes.
26. Serve hot with onion raita.

Note :

You can cook and serve this biryani in an ovenproof dish.

If you want, you can finish the biryani in a microwave oven also.

In that case cook covered on micro high for four minutes only.

13. SPICY MUTTON PULAO

Ingredients

4 cups basmati rice, soaked for ½ hour

4 tsps ginger paste

100 gms mutton

1 tbsp garlic paste

6 green chillies

1 onion, finely chopped

2 tomatoes, finely chopped

10 gms each cinnamon, cloves, cardamom

4 cups thick coconut milk

100 gms cashewnuts

200 gms ghee

2 tsps garam masala powder

3 tsps chilli powder

mint leaves and coriander leaves

½ tsp lemon juice

Method

1. Add ghee to a pan and fry the onions and tomatoes.
2. Grind the cashewnuts, cloves, cinnamon, cardamom, green chillies mint and coriander leaves.
3. Add the mixture to the ghee.
4. Add the ginger and garlic paste to it.
5. Then add the garam masala, chilli powder and mutton to it.
6. Add the coconut milk to the mixture, and salt to taste.
7. Bring the mixture to a boil and add the rice.
8. Add the lemon juice it and then allow the rice to be cooked.
9. Serve hot.

14. NAWABI PULAO

Ingredients

325 gms basmati rice

½ kg mutton, cut in pieces

3 onions, sliced

½ tbsp ginger-garlic paste

1 tsp garam masala

3 red chilies

1" cinnamon

½ cup curd, beaten

3 green cardamoms

5 peppers

5 cloves

½ tsp shahjeera

½ tsp turmeric powder

1 pinch saffron

¼ cup milk coriander/mint, chopped

5 apricots

dry fruits as required

ghee as required

Method

1. Fry the dry fruits and apricots in 2½ tbsps ghee with a little salt to taste.
2. Now grind the fried onions and red chillies to a fine paste.
3. Marinate the mutton pieces with curd, ginger-garlic paste, onion paste, turmeric powder and salt.
4. In a pressure cooker heat the ghee, add the marinated mutton and pressure cook till done.
5. Heat the ghee again in another vessel, add the whole spices, fry for a while and then add the washed rice.
6. Add the salt and warm water so that the level comes 1½ inches above the rice.
7. Cook till the rice is done.
8. Remove, spread out to cool and remove the whole spices.
9. Now to assemble, apply ghee to a heavy-bottomed vessel, add the cooked mutton and sprinkle a little garam masala.
10. Cover with a layer of rice, followed by melted ghee and then the saffron milk. Lastly, add the fried nuts, cover tightly and keep on dum for 15-20 minutes.
11. Mix and serve hot, garnished with chopped coriander and mint.

15. TROPICAL PRAWN PULAO

Ingredients

¼ kg rice,washed

150 gms prawns, cut into pieces

3 onions, chopped and fried

1 tbsp ginger-garlic paste

150 gms capsicum, cut

¼ kg tomatoes, chopped in strips

½ bunch coriander, chopped

1 spring onion, chopped

½ tsp saffron, soaked in water

1 tin pineapple slices, cubed

2 tbsps ghee

2 tbsps rice powder (cardamom,clove, cinnamon,

shahjeera,nutmeg, mace)

salt to taste

Method

1. Clean and rinse the rice.
2. Fry the chopped onions and keep aside.
3. Heat ghee in a vessel, fry the ginger-garlic paste till it changes colour, then add the prawns, salt and mix well.
4. When the prawns change colour remove from the pan, set aside and now add the vegetables in the same pan.
5. Fry for a while, then add the rice, salt and cook till the rice is done.
6. Take a vessel, put a layer of half the cooked rice, then sprinkle some saffron water followed by a layer of cooked prawns and some spice powder.

7. Then put some chopped pineapples and fried onions.
8. Repeat these layers once more ending with fried onions as the topmost layer.
9. Put some pineapple syrup all over the rice, cover and keep on dum for 15 minutes or more.
10. Remove and serve hot.

16. FISH PULAO

Ingredients

300 gms rice basmati

600 gms fish, without bones

2 bay leaves

¼ cup sliced onion

1 tbsp coriander leaves

1 tbsp fresh grated coconut

50 ml coconut milk

1 tsp lemon juice

½ tsp turmeric powder

2 green chillies

1 tsp whole garam masala

2 tbsps ghee/oil

salt as per taste

Method

1. Pick, wash and soak the rice for about 20 minutes.
2. Drain and keep aside.
3. Clean and wash the fish cut into small pieces.
4. Heat the ghee or oil in a thick-bottomed pan.
5. Add bay leaves and whole garam masala. Let it crackle.

6. Add the sliced onion, sauté till the onion turns pink.
7. Add water, turmeric powder, lemon juice and green chillies slit into two.
8. Bring it to a boil and add the rice.
9. Cook for a minute and add the prawns and coconut milk.
10. Season with salt.
11. Stir till the rice absorbs all the water and then cover it with a lid and cook on a slow fire till the rice and fish are fully cooked.
12. Garnish with chopped coriander leaves and grated fresh coconut.

17. ARABIAN PULAO

Ingredients

1 chicken raw or ¾ kg boiled mutton

3 medium-size fresh tomatoes, chopped

1 big onion, chopped

2 tsps cuminseeds, roasted slightly and ground

1 tbsp cinnamon powder

salt

crushed garlic and ginger paste

7 tbsps oil

3 tbsps ghee

2 cups basmati rice

few whole peppercorns

3 bay leaves

2 cardamoms

4 cups water

6 small potatoes, cut into halves

Method

1. Heat the oil/ghee.
2. Fry the onions slightly, then add the whole peppercorns, cardamom and bay leaves.
3. When the onions are slightly brown add the fresh tomatoes and the cumin-cinnamon powder.
4. Fry till the oil comes up, then add the raw chicken and potatoes.
5. When the chicken is half done measure in 4 cups of water.
6. When the water starts boiling add the rice and salt.
7. When rice is done bake it in the oven for 30 minutes at 150^{0}C.
8. Serve with salad and yogurt.

18. LAMB BIRIYANI

Ingredients

½ kg lamb

2 cups basmati rice

2 tsps chilli powder

½ tsp salt

1tsp coriander powder

½ tsp turmeric powder

1 tsp fresh ginger-garlic paste

1 tsp garam masala powder

4-5 bay leaves

5-6 cloves

1 tsp cumin

1 big onion

2 tsps curd

2 tbsps oil

Method

1. Cut the lamb into 10-12 pieces.
2. Add the ginger-garlic paste, turmeric, chilli powder, coriander powder, salt and garam masala.
3. Mix it together and keep it for 1 hour.
4. Cut onions vertically.
5. In a pressure pan heat the oil.
6. Add the cloves, bay leaves, jeera, onions, cashews. Fry them until red.
7. Add the marinated lamb to it and fry for 10-15 minutes.
8. Add the rice.
9. Fry for some time, then add 3 cups of water and pressure cook till the lamb is tender and done.

19. GOSHT BIRIYANI

Ingredients

1 kg mutton or lamb

2 cups basmati rice, washed

1 tbsp whole garam masala

2 cups yogurt

2 cups sliced onions

5 tbsps ghee or oil

2 green chillies, chopped

2 tbsps ginger paste

2 tbsps garlic paste

2 cups chopped tomatoes

salt to taste

1 tsp turmeric powder

2 tbsps coriander powder

1 tbsp cumin powder

1 tsp chilli powder

2 tbsps garam masala powder

a generous pinch of saffron

½ cup warm milk

2" ginger

½ cup chcpped coriander leaves

½ cup chopped mint leaves

50 gms butter

For the Garnishing

fried sliced onion

Method

1. Clean the mutton or lamb and cut into one and half inch-sized pieces.
2. Soak rice in water.
3. Soak the saffron in warm milk and keep aside.
4. Marinade the meat pieces with yogurt, salt, turmeric powder and one tablespoon each of ginger and garlic pastes.
5. Marinade for about four hours in a cool place.
6. Cook the rice in salted boiling water along with whole garam masala till rice is almost cooked.
7. Strain and keep the rice warm.
8. Heat ghee or oil in a thick-bottomed pan or pressure cooker.
9. Add the onions and chillies.
10. Cook till the onion is light golden brown.

11. Make sure to stir continuously.
12. Add the remaining ginger and garlic pastes and mix well.
13. Add the marinated meat and cook on high flame for seven to eight minutes.
14. Now, add the coriander powder, cumin powder and chilli powder.
15. Mix thoroughly.
16. Stir in three cups of water, bring it to a boil, reduce heat and cook covered till meat pieces are almost cooked.
17. Add the chopped tomatoes, salt, one teaspoon garam masala powder and chopped fresh coriander leaves.
18. Cook for fifteen minutes on medium heat, stirring occasionally.
19. In case you are cooking meat in the pressure cooker, add chopped tomatoes, salt, garam masala powder, two cups of water and chopped fresh coriander leaves after adding dry spices.
20. Pressure cook till meat pieces are almost cooked.
21. It normally takes two or three whistles to cook the meat.
22. Ensure that the cooked meat does not have a runny gravy.
23. In that the case, cook on high flame to reduce the water content.
24. Arrange half the quantity of cooked meat in an ovenproof dish and spread half the quantity of cooked rice on top of the meat.
25. Sprinkle a little garam masala powder, half the amount each of ginger julienne, saffron dissolved in warm milk and mint leaves.
26. Dot the rice with half the quantity of butter.
27. Place a layer of remaining meat on top of the rice, followed by cooked rice and repeat the earlier process with the remaining quantities of ginger julienne, saffron milk, garam masala powder, mint leaves and butter.

28. Cover it with aluminium foil and cook in a pre-heated oven for fifteen to twenty minutes.
29. Serve garnished with fried sliced onions and mixed vegetable raita.

20. CHICKEN BRIYANI

Ingredients

2 cups basmati rice

¾ kg chicken pieces

½ cup milk

1 cup yogurt

3 onions, thinly sliced

1 tsp ginger paste

½ tsp garlic paste

1 tsp green chilli paste

½ cup tomato puree

2 tsps chilli powder

1 tsp turmeric powder

1 tsp roasted cumin powder

2 tsps garam masala powder

½ tsp cardamom powder

a pinch of saffron

1 tsp coriander powder

2 tbsps coriander leaves

salt to taste

7 tbsps vegetable oil

Method

1. Mix the tomato puree, yogurt, ginger-garlic paste, green chilli paste, chilli powder, turmeric powder, roasted cumin powder, garam masala, coriander powder and salt.

2. Stir well. Marinate the chicken with this mixture and keep aside for 3-4 hours.
3. Heat oil in a pan.
4. Fry the onions until golden brown.
5. Add the marinated chicken and cook for 10 minutes.
6. Add 4 cups of water to the rice.
7. Mix saffron in milk and add to it.
8. Add the cardamom powder.
9. Add the chicken pieces.
10. Pressure cook the rice. Mix gently.
11. Garnish with green coriander leaves and serve hot.

DESSERTS

DESSERTS

1. APPLE SPICE CAKE

Ingredients

2 cups sugar

3 cups flour

2 apples

2 tsps powdered cinnamon

½ tsp nutmeg

½ tsp ginger powder

pinch of clove powder

1 tsp vanilla essence

1 tsp almond essence

½ tsp baking powder

3 eggs

1 cup oil

Method

1. Mix the flour, sugar, oil and baking powder with a pinch of salt in a food processor.
2. Mix well.

3. Add egg one at a time in the food processor while running it. Mix well.
4. Take out the dough and add all the ingredients except apples.
5. You may peel the apples or they can be just cut into small pieces.
6. Mix the apples with the hand as the dough will be hard.
7. Press by hand.
8. Grease the pan and bake at 180 degrees for one hour or till a needle inserted in the cake comes out clean.

2. BREAD PUDDING

Ingredients for the Pudding

16 slices white plain sweet bread, crust sliced off

3 small eggs

2½ cups milk

2 cups sugar

2 tbsps raisins

2 tbsps walnuts, chopped

2 tbsps cashewnuts, chopped

1 tsp vanilla essence

candied cherries for garnish

Ingredients for Custard Topping

2 tbsps custard powder, dissolved in warm milk

2 cups milk

1 cup sugar

Method

1. Blend the sugar, milk, essence and eggs for the pudding in the blender to get a smooth liquid.
2. Grease a rectangular deep pan with butter or oil and place 8 slices of bread to cover the bottom.
3. Sprinkle one tablespoon each of the raisins/nuts on it.
4. Now pour the blended egg/milk mixture on top of it.
5. Place a second layer of the remaining 8 bread slices, sprinkle the remaining nuts/raisins and pour the remaining mixture on it.
6. Bake in an oven for about 35 minutes at 375° F till done.
7. When tested with a thin knife (toothpick), the knife (toothpick) should come out clean.
8. Take it out and cool for 10 minutes.
9. For the custard topping heat the sugar and milk.
10. When the sugar dissolves completely, add the custard and keep stirring till it thickens.
11. Take it off the fire and let it cool for 10 minutes.
12. Pour this custard mixture on top of the baked dish and let it chill in the fridge for 2 hours.
13. Cut it into slices and garnish with candied cherry or two.

3. CARAMEL PUDDING

Ingredients

1 egg

1 cup milk

2 tbsps sugar

a few drops of vanilla essence

Method

1. In a baking pan that fits into the cooker sprinkle 5-6 teaspoons of sugar.
2. Hold it over a small flame until the sugar starts to caramelise.
3. Then spread the caramel evenly over the dish so that it covers the entire base of the dish.
4. Remove and keep aside to cool.
5. Boil the milk in a pan and set aside till it cools to room temp.
6. Take a wide mixing bowl and beat the egg using an electric hand mixer until it gets foamy.
7. Then blend in the sugar and beat it once more.
8. Now add the cooled milk slowly to the mixture and blend well.
9. Add a few drops of vanilla essence to the mixture and blend again.
10. Now pour this mixture into the baking dish on the cooled caramel layer.
11. Pour 2 inches of water into the cooker and place the dish into it.
12. Steam it for a good 15 minutes on low flame with the weight on.
13. Once it is done remove the dish and set aside for cooling.
14. Then place it in the refrigerator for 2 hour.
15. Before serving cut the entire edge of the pudding along the sides using a knife in order to loosen it.
16. Then cover the dish with an upturned plate and overturn the dish so that the pudding slides on to the plate.
17. Cut and serve.

4. DATE DELIGHT

Ingredients

150 gms dates, chopped

250 ml boiling water

¼ tsp soda bicarbonate

60 gms butter

200 gms sugar

1 egg

¼ tsp vanilla

225 gms all-purpose flour

¼ tsp baking powder

a pinch of salt

50 gms nuts

Method

1. Pour boiling water on the chopped dates and add soda bicarbonate.
2. Beat the butter and sugar together, add the egg and vanilla and beat well.
3. Sift the flour, baking powder and salt and fold alternately with the date mixture into the creamed butter, sugar and egg.
4. Add the chopped nuts and stir well.
5. Pour the batter into a pie dish and bake in a pre-heated oven for 30-40 minutes at 180°C.
6. Remove and let it cool completely before making slices.

5. FRIED ICE CREAM

Ingredients for the Batter

2 cups ice cream

sponge cake

oil to deep fry

1 cup maida

1 egg

1 cup milk

fruit slices

Method

1. Make balls of hard frozen ice cream.
2. Wrap each ball in thick sponge cake tightly and freeze these balls.
3. Deep fry the hard frozen balls just until the batter is solid.
4. Serve immediately on a platter of fruit slices.

6. LEMON BARS

Ingredients for the Crust

1 cup soft butter

½ cup powdered sugar

2 cups flour

salt

Ingredients for the Top Layer

4 eggs, beaten

¼ cup flour

2 cups granulated sugar

6 tbsps lemon juice

grated rind of 2 lemons

Method

1. Combine the ingredients for the crust and mix well.
2. Press the mixture in 9 x 13-inch greased pan.
3. Bake at 350° F for 15 minutes or until lightly browned.
4. For the top layer, combine the flour and sugar.
5. Mix in the beaten eggs, lemon juice and rind.
6. Pour onto slightly cooled crust.
7. Bake at 350° F for 25 minutes or until the filling is set.
8. Cool and sprinkle with powdered sugar.

7. CHERRY WHIRLS

Ingredients

1 cup flour

½ cup castor sugar

⅓ cup chilled ghee

½ egg

2 tbsps milk powder

a few drops vanilla

lemon essence

a few cherries

a big star nozzle

milk according to need

Method

1. Cream the ghee and sugar till creamy.
2. Add the egg and essence and beat for a minute, then add all the dry ingredients.
3. Add the milk to thicken but not to very thick consistency like that of a dough.
4. Grease a baking tray and pipe stars on it. Stick a cherry on each.
5. Bake in moderate oven for 10 to 12 minutes or till golden.
6. Remove and cool on a wire rack.

8. CREME BRULEE

Ingredients

4 egg yolks

4 tbsps castor sugar

1 ½ cups cream

½ tsp vanilla or

lemon essence

½ lemon rind

Method

1. Beat the egg yolks in a bowl.
2. Add 2 tbsps castor sugar and cream to the egg mixture and keep over a pan of hot water, stirring constantly till the boiling point is reached.
3. Remove the pan from heat.
4. Add the essence and lemon rind and chill until firm.
5. Now sprinkle the leftover sugar on it and keep under the grill till the top is brown.
6. Return to refrigerator to chill again.

Other Books on

HEALTH

1. Ayurveda For All **(New)** 150/-
2. A Guide To Migraine, Airthritis, Cervical Spondylosis and Backache **(New)** 125/-
3. Body and Beauty Care **(New)** 125/-
4. Yoga For All 250/-
5. Child Care & Nutrition **(New)** 95/-
6. Naturopathy Modern Way of Life 125/-
7. A Guide to Your Pregnancy 150/-
8. First Aid How to Handle an Accident 125/-
9. Acupressure in Daily Life 125/-
10. Complete Book of Yoga 150/-
11. Look Younger at Any Age 125/-
12. HIV/AIDS - Transmission, Prevention and A. Therapies 110/-
13. Diabetics And Diet 110/-
14. Increase Your Height and Loose Your Weight 125/-
15. Make Fitness A Way of Life 195/-
16. Common Problems of Children 150/-
17. Handbook of Nutrition & Dietetics 250/-
18. A Guide To Massage Therapy 125/-
19. A Guide To Family Medicine 150/-
20. A Guide To Digestive Disorders 125/-

21.	Complete Book of Child Care	150/-
22.	A Guide to Homoeopathy	125/-
23.	Life Begins at 40	125/-
24.	Alternative Therapies	125/-
25.	How to Overcome Stress	125/-
26.	Yoga Therapy	225/-
27.	Obesity	125/-
28.	Self Motivation	125/-
29.	Yoga For Health And Relaxation	110/-
30.	Women Disorders and Pregnancy	110/-
31.	A Guide To Body Pains	95/-
32.	Sex Education	95/-
33.	Common Diseases and Cure	95/-
34.	Pranayama For Better Life	110/-
35.	Herbal Home Remedies	110/-
36.	A Guide to Beauty & Skin Care	95/-
37.	A Guide to Heart Care	95/-
38.	A Guide to High Blood Pressure	90/-
39.	Cancer Causes and Prevention	110/-
40.	Nature Cure For Common Diseases	110/-
41.	Good Health Through Food & Regimen	90/-
42.	A Guide to Allergies	125/-
43.	A Guide to Aging	95/-
44.	Ayurveda for Health & Beauty	95/-

Unit No. 220, Second Floor, 4735/22,
Prakash Deep Building,Ansari Road, Daryaganj,
New Delhi- 110002, Ph.: 32903912, 23280047, 09811838000
• E-mail : lotus_press@sify.com. www.lotuspress.co.in